A Theological Study In Exodus

A Spiritual Enlightenment

**Arch Bishop
D A Miller D.D.; PhD.**

Copyright ©1982, 2011
Roseville, Michigan
USA

© 1982, 2011 by Arch-Bishop D.A. Miller D.D.: Founder and Presiding Prelate.

All Rights Reserved.

No part of this book may be reproduced, stored in a retrieval system or transmitted in any form or by any means except for pre-paid e-book transactions without the prior written permission of the author, except by a reviewer who may quote brief passages in a review to be printed in a newspaper, magazine or journal.

Third Printing

Showers of Blessings Ministries International Publishing has allowed this work to remain exactly as the author intended, verbatim, without editorial input.

PUBLISHED BY

SHOWERS OF BLESSINGS MINISTRIES INTERNATIONAL PUBLISHING

www.showersofblessings.us

Roseville, MI

THE NAMES ON AARON'S BREASTPLATE

Aaron shall bear their names before the Lord, upon his two shoulders, for a memorial.... And Aaron shall bear the names of the Children of Israel in the breastplate of judgment upon his heart, when he goeth in unto the Holy Place.'—Exodus 28:12, 29.

Every part of the elaborately prescribed dress of the high priest was significant. But the significance of the whole was concentrated in the inscription upon his MITRE, 'Holiness to the Lord,' and in those others upon his breastplate and his shoulder.

The breastplate was composed of folded cloth, in which was lodged twelve precious stones, in four rows of three, each stone containing the name of one of the tribes. It was held in position by the ephod, which consisted of another piece of cloth, with a back and front part, which were united into one on the shoulders.

On each shoulder it was clasped by an onyx stone bearing the names of six of the tribes. Thus twice, on the shoulders, the seat of power, and on the heart, the organ of thought and of love, Aaron, entering into the presence of the Most High, bore 'the names of the tribes for a memorial continually.'

Now, I think we shall not be indulging in the very dangerous amusement of unduly spiritualizing the externalities of that old law if we see here, in these two things, some very important lessons.

The first one that I would suggest to you is—here we have the expression of the great truth of representation of the people by the priest.

The names of the tribes laid upon Aaron's heart and on his shoulders indicated the significance of his office—that he represented Israel before God, as truly as he represented God to Israel.

For the moment the personality of the official was altogether melted away and absorbed in the sanctity of his function, and he stood before God as the individualized nation. Aaron was Israel, and Israel was Aaron, for the purposes of worship. And that was indicated by the fact that here, on the shoulders from which, according to an obvious symbol, all acts of power emanate, and on the heart from which, according to most natural metaphor, all the outgoings of the personal life proceed, were written the names of the tribes. That meant, 'This man standing here is the Israel of God, the concentrated nation.'

The same thought works the other way. The nation is the diffused priest, and all its individual components are consecrated to God. All this was external ceremonial, with no real spiritual fact at the back of it. But it pointed onwards to something that is not ceremonial.

It pointed to this, that the true priest must, in like manner, gather up into himself, and in a very profound sense be, the people for whom he is the priest; and that they, in their turn, by the action of their own minds and hearts and wills, must consent to and recognize that representative relation, which comes to the solemn height of identification in Christ's relation to His people. 'I am the Vine, ye are the branches,' says He, and also, 'That they all may be one in us as Thou,

Father, art in Me, and I in Thee.' So Paul says, 'I live, yet not I, but Christ liveth in me.' 'The life which I live in the flesh, I live by the faith of the Son of God,'

So Christ gathers us all, if we will let Him, into Himself; and our lives may be hid with Him—in a fashion that is more than mere external and formal representation, or as people have a member of Parliament to represent them in the councils of the nation—even in a true union with Him in whom is the life of all of us, if we live in any real sense. Aaron bore the names of the tribes on shoulder and heart, and Israel was Aaron, and Aaron was Israel. Further, we see here, in these eloquent symbols, the true significance of intercession.

Now, that is a word and a thought which has been wrongfully limited and made shallow and superficial by the unfortunate confining of the expression, in our ordinary language, to a mere action by speech. Intercession is supposed to be verbal asking for some good to be bestowed on, or some evil to be averted from, some one in whom we are interested. But the Old Testament notion of the priest's intercession, and the New Testament use of the word which we so render, go far beyond any verbal utterances, and reach to the very heart of things. Intercession, in the true sense of the word, means the doing of any act whatsoever before God for His people by Jesus Christ.

When-so-ever, as in the presence of God, He brings to God anything which is His, that is intercession. He undertakes for them, not by words only, though His mighty word is, 'I will that they whom Thou hast given Me, be with Me where I am,' but by acts which are more than even the words of the Incarnate Word.

If we take these two inscriptions upon which I am now commenting, we shall get, I think, what covers the whole ground of the intercession on which Christians are to repose their souls. For, with regard to the one of them, we read that the high priest's breastplate was named 'the breastplate of judgment'; and what that means is explained by the last words of the verse following that from which my text is taken: 'Aaron shall bear the judgment of the children of Israel upon his heart before the Lord.' Judgment means a judicial sentence; in this case a judicial sentence of acquittal. And that Aaron stood before God in the Holy Place, ministering with this breastplate upon his heart, is explained by the writer of these regulations to mean that he carried there the visible manifestation of Israel's acquittal, based upon his own sacrificial function. Now, put that into plain English, and it is just this—Jesus Christ's sacrifice ensures, for all those whose names are written on these gems on His heart, their acquittal in the judgment of Heaven.

Or, in other words, the first step in the intercession of our great High Priest is the presenting before God forever and ever that great fact that He, the Sinless, has died for the love of sinful men, and thereby has secured that the judgment of Heaven on them shall now be 'no condemnation.' Brethren, there is the root of all our hope in Christ, and of all that Christ is to individuals and to society—the assurance that the breastplate of judgment is on His heart, as a sign that all who trust Him are acquitted by the tribunal of Heaven. The other side of this great continual act of intercession is set forth by the other symbol—the names written on the shoulders, the seat of power. There is a beautiful parallel, which yet at first sight does not seem to be one, to the thought that lies here, in the Book of the Prophet Isaiah, where, addressing the restored and perfected Israel, he says, speaking in the person of Jehovah: 'I have graven thee upon the palms of My hands.' That has precisely the same meaning that I take to be conveyed by this symbol in the text. The names of the tribes are written on His shoulders; and not until that arm is wearied or palsied, not till that strong hand forgets its cunning, will our defiance fail. If our names are thus written on the seat of power, that means that all the divine authority and omnipotence which Jesus Christ, the Eternal Son of the Father, wields in His state of royal glory, are exercised on behalf of, or at all events on the side of, those whose names He thus bears upon His shoulders.

That is the guarantee for each of us that our hands shall be made strong, according to the ancient prophetic blessing, 'by the hands of the mighty God of Jacob.' Just as a father or a mother will take their child's little tremulous hand in theirs and hold it, that it may be strengthened for some small task beyond its unbacked, uninvigorated power; so Jesus Christ will give us strength within, and also will order the march of His Providence and send the gift of His Spirit, for the succor and the strengthening of all whose names are written on His ephod. He has gone within the veil. He has left us heavy tasks, but our names are on His shoulders, and we 'can do all things in Christ who strengthened us.' Still further, this symbol suggests to us the depth and reality of Christ's sympathy.

The heart is, in our language, the seat of love. It is not so in the Old Testament. Affection is generally allocated to another part of the frame; but here the heart stands for the organ of care, of thought, of interest. For, according to the Old Testament view of the relation between man's body and man's soul, the very seat and centre of the individual life is in the heart. I suppose that was because it was known that, somehow or other, the blood came thence. Be that as it may, the thought is clear throughout all the Old Testament that the heart is the man, and the man is the heart. And so, if Jesus bears our names upon His heart, that does not express merely representation nor merely intercession, but it expresses also personal regard, individualizing knowledge. For Aaron wore not one great jewel with 'Israel' written on it, but twelve little ones, with 'Dan,' 'Benjamin,' and 'Ephraim,' and all the rest of them, each on his own gem.

So we can say, 'Such a High Priest became us, who could have compassion upon the ignorant, and upon them that are out of the way'; and we can fall back on that old-fashioned but inexhaustible source of consolation and strength: 'In all their affliction He was afflicted'; and though the noise of the tempests which toss us can scarcely be supposed to penetrate into the veiled place where He dwells on high, yet we may be sure—and take all the peace and consolation and encouragement out of it that it is meant to give us—that 'we have not a High Priest that cannot be touched with a feeling of our infirmities,' but that Himself, having known miseries, 'is able to succor them that are tempted.' Our names are on Christ's heart. Then, lastly, we have here a suggestion of how precious to Aaron Israel is.

Jewels were chosen to symbolize the tribes. Bits of tin, potsherds, or anything else that one could have scratched letters upon, would have done quite as well. But 'the precious things of the everlasting mountains' were chosen to bear the dear names. 'The Lord's portion is His people'; and precious in the eyes of Christ are the souls for whom He has given so much. They are not only precious, but lustrous, flashing back the light in various colors indeed, according to their various laws of crystallization, but all receptive of it and all reflective of it. I said that the names on the breastplate of judgment expressed the acquittal and acceptance of Israel. But does Christ's work for us stop with simple acquittal? Oh no! 'Whom He justified them He also glorified,' And if our souls are 'bound in the bundle of life,' and our names are written on the heart of the Christ, be sure that mere forgiveness and acquittal is the least of the blessings which He intends to give, and that He will not be satisfied until in all our nature we receive and flash back the light of His own glory.

It is very significant in this aspect that the names of the twelve tribes are described as being written on the precious stones which make the walls of the New Jerusalem. Thus borne on Christ's heart whilst He is within the veil and we are in the outer courts, we may hope to be carried by His sustaining and perfecting hand into the glories, and be made participant of the glories. Let us see to it that we write His name on our hearts, on their cares, their thought, their love, and on our hands, on their toiling and their possessing; and then, God helping us, and Christ dwelling in us, we shall come to the blessed state of those who serve Him, and bear His name flaming conspicuous for ever on their foreheads.

THREE INSCRIPTIONS WITH ONE MEANING

'Thou shalt make a plate of pure gold, and grave upon it ... HOLINESS TO THE LORD.'—Exodus 28:36.

'In that day there shall be upon the bells of the horses, HOLINESS UNTO THE LORD.'—Zechariah 14:20.

'His name shall be in their foreheads.'—Revelation 22:4.

You will have perceived my purpose in putting these three widely separated texts together. They all speak of inscriptions, and they are all obviously connected with each other. The first of them comes from the ancient times of the institution of the ceremonial ritual, and describes a part of the high priest's official dress. In his MITRE was a thin plate of gold on which was written, 'Holiness to the Lord.' The second of them comes from almost the last portion recorded of the history of Israel in the Old Testament, and is from the words of the great Prophet of the Restoration—his ideal presentation of the Messianic period, in which he recognizes as one feature, that the inscription on the MITRE of the high priest shall be written on 'the bells of the horses.' And the last of them is from the closing vision of the celestial kingdom, the heavenly and perfected form of the Christian Church. John, probably remembering the high priest and his MITRE, with its inscription upon the forehead, says: 'His servants shall do Him priestly service'—for that is the meaning of the word inadequately translated 'serve Him'—'and see His face, and His name shall be in their foreheads.'

These three things, then—the high priest's MITRE, the horses' bells, the foreheads of the perfected saints—present three aspects of the Christian thought of holiness. Take them one by one.

I. The high priest's MITRE.

The high priest was the official representative of the nation. He stood before God as the embodied and personified Israel. For the purposes of worship Israel was the high priest, and the high priest was Israel. And so, on his forehead, not to distinguish him from the rest of the people, but to include all the people in his consecration, shone a golden plate with the motto, 'Holiness to the Lord.' So, at the very beginning of Jewish ritual there stands a protest against all notions that make 'saint' the designation of any abnormal or exceptional sanctity, and confine the name to the members of any selected aristocracy of devoutness and goodness. All Christian men, *ex officio*, by the very fact of their Christianity, are saints, in the true sense of the word. And the representative of the whole of Israel stood there before God, with this inscription blazing on his forehead, as a witness that, whatsoever holiness may be, it belongs to every member of the true Israel.

And what is it? It is a very unfortunate thing—indicating superficiality of thought—that the modern popular notion of 'holiness' identifies it with purity, righteousness, moral perfection. Now that idea *is* in it, but is not the whole of it. For, not to spend time upon mere remarks on words, the meaning of the word thus rendered is in Hebrew, as well as in Greek and in our own English, one and the same. The root-meaning is 'separated,' 'set apart,' and the word expresses primarily, not moral character, but relation to God. That makes all the difference; and it incalculably deepens the conception, as well as puts us on the right track for understanding the only possible means by which there can ever be realized that moral perfection and excellence which has unfortunately monopolized the meaning of the word in most people's minds. The first thought is 'set apart to God.' That is holiness, in its root and germ.

And how can we be set apart for God? You may devote a dead thing for certain uses easily enough. How can a man be separated and laid aside?

Well, there is only one way, brethren, and that is by self-surrender. 'Yield yourselves to God' is but the other side, or, rather, the practical shape, of the Old and the New Testament doctrine of holiness. A man becomes God's when he says, 'Lord, take me and mould me, and fill me and cleanse me, and do with me what Thou wilt.' In that self-surrender, which is the tap-root of all holiness, the first and foremost thing to be offered is that most obstinate of all, the will that is in us. And when we yield our wills in submission both to commandments and providences, both to gifts and to withdrawals, both to gains and to losses, both to joys and to sorrows, then we begin to write upon our foreheads 'Holiness to the Lord.' And when we go on to yield our hearts to Him, by enshrining Him sole and sovereign in their innermost chamber, and turning to Him the whole current of our lives and desires, and hopes and confidences, which we are so apt to allow to run to waste and be sucked up in the desert sands of the world, then we write more of that inscription. And when we fill our minds with joyful submission to His truth, and occupy our thoughts with His mighty Name and His great revelation, and carry Him with us in the hidden corners of our consciousness, even whilst we are busy about daily work, then we add further letters to it. And when the submissive will, and the devoted heart, and the occupied thoughts are fully expressed in daily life and its various external duties, then the writing is complete. 'Holiness to the Lord' is self-surrender of will and heart and mind and everything. And that surrender is of the very essence of Christianity.

What is a saint? Some man or woman that has practiced unheard-of austerities? Somebody that has lived an isolated and self-regarding life in convent or monastery or desert? No! a man or woman in the world who, moved by the mercies of God, yields self to God as 'a living sacrifice.' So the New Testament writers never hesitate to speak even of such very imperfect Christians as were found in abundance in churches like Corinth and Galatia as being all 'saints,' every man of them. That is not because the writers were minimizing their defects, or idealizing their persons, but because, if they are Christians at all, they are saints; seeing that no man is a Christian who has not been drawn by Christ's great sacrifice for him to yield himself a sacrifice for Christ.

Of course that intrusive idea which has, in popular apprehension, so swallowed up the notion of holiness—viz. that of perfection of moral character or conduct—is included in this other, or rather is developed from it. For the true way to conquer self is to surrender self; and the more entire our giving up of ourselves, the more certainly shall we receive ourselves back again from His hands. 'By the mercies of God, I beseech you, yield yourselves living sacrifices.'

II. I come to my next text—the horses' bells.

Zechariah has a vision of the ideal Messianic times, and, of course, as must necessarily be the case, his picture is painted with colors laid upon his palette by his experience, and he depicts that distant future in the guise suggested to him by what he saw around him. So we have to disentangle from his words the sentiment which he expresses, and to recognize the symbolic way in which he puts it. His thought is this,—the inscription on the high priest's MITRE will be written on the bells which ornament the harness of the horses, which in Israel were never used as with us, but only either for war or for pomp and display, and the use of which was always regarded with a certain kind of doubt and suspicion. Even these shall be consecrated in that far-off day. And then he goes on with variations on the same air, 'In that day there shall be upon the bells of the horses, "Holiness unto the Lord,"' and adds that 'the pots in the Lord's house'—the humble vessels that were used for the most ordinary parts of the Temple services—'shall be like the bowls before the altar,' into which the sacred blood of the offerings was poured. The most external and secular thing bearing upon religion shall be as sacred as the sacredness. But that is not all. 'Yea! every pot in Jerusalem and in Judah shall be holiness unto the Lord of hosts, and all they that sacrifice shall come and take of them,' and put their offerings therein. That is to say, the coarse pottery vessels that were in every poverty-stricken house in the city shall be elevated to the rank of the sacred vessels of the Temple. Domestic life with all its secularities shall be hallowed. The kitchens of Jerusalem shall be as truly places of worship as is the inner shrine of the Most High.

On the whole, the prophet's teaching is that, in the ideal state of man upon earth, there will be an entire abolition of the distinction between 'sacred' and 'secular'; a distinction that has wrought infinite mischief in the world, and in the lives of Christian people. Let me translate these words of our prophet into English equivalents. Every cup and tumbler in a poor man's kitchen may be as sacred as the communion chalice that passes from lip to lip with the 'blood of Jesus Christ' in it. Every common piece of service that we do, down among the vulgarities and the secularities and the meanness's of daily life, may be lifted up to stand upon precisely the same level as the scariest office that we undertake. The bells of the horses may jingle to the same tune as the trumpets of the priests sounded within the shrine, and on all, great and small, may be written, 'Holiness to the Lord.'

But let us remember that that universally diffused sanctity will need to have a centre of diffusion, else there will be no diffusion, and that all life will become sacred when the man that lives it has 'Holiness to the Lord' written on his forehead, and not else. If that be the inscription on the driver's heart, the horses that he drives will have it written on their bells, but they will not have it unless it be. Holy men make all things holy. 'To the pure all things are pure,' but unto them that are unclean and disobedient there is nothing pure. Hallow thyself, and all things are clean unto thee.

III. And so I come to my third text—the perfected saints' foreheads.

The connection between the first and the last of these texts is as plain and close as between the first and the second. For John in his closing vision gives emphasis to the priestly idea as designating in its deepest relations the redeemed and perfected Christian Church. Therefore he says, as I have already explained, 'His servants shall do Him *priestly* service, and His name shall be in their foreheads.' The old official dress of the high priest comes into his mind, and he paints the future, just as Zechariah did, under the forms of the past, and sees before the throne the perfected saints, each man of them with that inscription clear and conspicuous.

But there is an advance in his words which I think it is not fanciful to note. It is only the *name* that is written in the perfected saint's forehead. Not the 'Holiness unto the Lord,' but just the bare name. What does that mean? Well, it means the same as your writing your name in one of your books does, or as when a man puts his initials on the back of his oxen, or as the old practice of branding the master's mark upon the slave did. It means absolute ownership. But it means something more. The name is the manifested personality, the revealed God, or, as we say in an abstract way, the character of God. That Name is to be in the foreheads of His perfected people. How does it come to be there? Read also the clause before the text—'His servants shall see His face, and His name shall be in their foreheads.' That is to say, the perfected condition is not reached by surrender only, but by assimilation; and that assimilation comes by contemplation. The faces that are turned to Him, and behold Him, are smitten with the light and shine, and those that look upon them see 'as it had been the face of an angel,' as the Sanhedrim saw that of Stephen, when he beheld the Son of Man 'standing at the right hand of God.'

My last text is but a picturesque way of saying what the writer of it says in plain words when he declares, 'We shall be like Him, for we shall see Him as He is.' The name is to be 'in their foreheads,' where every eye can see it. Alas! alas! it is so hard for us to live out our best selves, and to show to the world what is in us. Cowardice, sheepishness, and a hundred other reasons prevent it. In this poor imperfect state no emotion ever takes shape and visibility without losing more or less of its beauty. But yonder the obstructions to self-manifestation will be done away; and 'when He shall be manifested, we also shall be manifested with Him in glory.' 'Then shall the righteous blaze forth like the sun in My heavenly Father's Kingdom.' But the beginning of it all is 'Holiness to the Lord' written on our hearts; and the end of that is the vision which is impossible without holiness, and which leads on to the beholder's perfect likeness to his Lord.

THE ALTAR OF INCENSE

'Thou shalt make an altar to burn incense upon.'
—Exodus 30:1.

    Ceremonies are embodied thoughts. Religious ceremonies are molded by, and seek to express, the worshipper's conception of his God, and his own relation to Him; his aspirations and his need. Of late years scholars have been busy studying the religions of the more backward races, and explaining rude and repulsive rites by pointing to the often profound and sometimes beautiful ideas underlying them. When that process is applied to Australian and Fijian savages, it is honored as a new and important study; when we apply it to the Mosaic Ritual it is pooh-poohed as 'foolish spiritualizing.' Now, no doubt, there has been a great deal of nonsense talked in regard to this matter, and a great deal of ingenuity wasted in giving a Christian meaning—or, may I say, a Christian twist?—to every pin of the Tabernacle, and every detail of the ritual. Of course, to exaggerate a truth is the surest way to discredit a truth, but the truth remains true all the same, and underneath that elaborate legislation, which makes such wearisome and profitless reading for the most of us, in the Pentateuch, there lie, if we can only grasp them, great thoughts and lessons that we shall all be the better for pondering.

To one item of these, this altar of incense, I call attention now, because it is rich in suggestions, and leads us into very sacred regions of the Christian life which are by no means so familiar to many of us as they ought to be. Let me just for one moment state the facts with which I wish to deal. The Jewish Tabernacle, and subsequently the Temple, were arranged in three compartments: the outermost court, which was accessible to all the people; the second, which was trodden by the priests alone; and the third, where the Shechinah dwelt in solitude, broken only once a year by the foot of the High Priest. That second court we are concerned with now. There are three pieces of ecclesiastical furniture in it: an altar in the centre, flanked on either side by a great lamp stand, and a table on which were piled loaves. It is to that central piece of furniture that I ask your attention now, and to the thoughts that underlie it, and the lessons that it teaches.

I. This altar shows us what prayer is.

Suppose we had been in that court when in the morning or in the evening the priest came with the glowing pan of coals from another altar in the outer court, and laid it on this altar, and heaped upon it the sticks of incense, we should have seen the curling, fragrant wreaths ascending till 'the House was filled with smoke,' as a prophet once saw it. We should not have wanted any interpreter to tell us what that meant. What could that rising cloud of sweet odors signify but the ascent of the soul towards God? Put that into more abstract words, and it is just the old, hackneyed commonplace which I seek to try to freshen a little now, that incense is the symbol of prayer. That that is so is plain enough, not only from the natural propriety of the case, but because you find the identification distinctly stated in several places in Scripture, of which I quote but two instances. In one psalm we read, 'Let my prayer come before Thee as incense.' In the Book of the Apocalypse we read of 'golden bowls full of odors, which are the prayers of saints.' And that the symbolism was understood by, and modified the practice of, the nation, we are taught when we read that whilst Zechariah the priest was within the court offering incense, as it was his lot to do, 'the whole multitude of the people were without praying,' doing that which the priest within the court symbolized by his offering. So then we come to this, dear friends, that we fearfully misunderstand and limit the nobleness and the essential character of prayer when, as we are always tempted to do by our inherent self-regard, we make petition its main feature and form. Of course, so long as we are what we shall always be in this world, needy and sinful creatures; and so long as we are what we shall ever be in all worlds, creatures absolutely dependent for life and everything on the will and energy of God, petition must necessarily be a very large part of prayer. But the more we grow into His likeness, and the more we understand the large privileges and the glorious possibilities which lie in prayer, the more will the relative proportions of its component parts be changed, and petition will become less, and aspiration will become more. The essence of prayer, the noblest form of it, is thus typified by the cloud of sweet odors that went up before God.

In all true prayer there must be the lowest prostration in reverence before the Infinite Majesty. But the noblest prayer is that which lifts 'them that are bowed down' rather than that which prostrates men before an inaccessible Deity. And so, whilst we lie low at His feet, that may be the prayer of a mere theist, but when our hearts go out towards Him, and we are drawn to Himself, that is the prayer that befits Christian aspiration; the ascent of the soul toward God is the true essence of prayer. As one of the non-Christian philosophers—seekers after God, if ever there were such, and who, I doubt not, found Him whom they sought—has put it, 'the flight of the lonely soul to the only God'; that is prayer. Is that my prayer? We come to Him many a time burdened with some very real sorrow, or weighted with some pressing responsibility, and we should not be true to ourselves, or to Him, if our prayer did not take the shape of petition. But, as we pray, the blessing of the transformation of its character should be realized by us, and that which began with the cry for help and deliverance should always be, and it always will be, if the cry for help and deliverance has been of the right sort, sublimed into 'Thy face, Lord, will I seek.' The Book of Ecclesiastes describes death as the 'return of the spirit to God who gave it.' That is the true description of prayer, a going back to the fountain's source. Flames aspire; to the place 'whence the rivers came thither they return again.' The homing pigeon or the migrating bird goes straight through many degrees of latitude, and across all sorts of weather, to the place whence it came. Ah! brethren, let us ask ourselves if our spirits thus aspire and soar. Do we know what it is to be, if I might so say, like those captive balloons that are ever yearning upwards, and stretching to the loftiest point permitted them by the cord that tethers them to earth?

Now another thought that this altar of incense may teach us is that the prayer that soars must be kindled. There is no fragrance in a stick of incense lying there. No wreaths of ascending smoke come from it. It has to be kindled before its sweet odor can be set free and ascend. That is why so much of our prayer is of no delight to God, and of no benefit to us, because it is not on fire with the flame of a heart kindled into love and thankfulness by the great sacrifice of Jesus Christ.

The cold vapors lie like a winding-sheet down in the valleys until the sun smites them, warms them, and draws them up. And our desires will hover in the low levels, and be dank and damp, until they are drawn up to the heights by the warmth of the Sun of righteousness. Oh! brethren, the formality and the coldness, to say nothing of the inconsecutiveness and the interruptedness by rambling thoughts that we all know in our petitions, in our aspirations, are only to be cured in one way:— 'Come! shed abroad a Savior's love, And that will kindle ours.'

It is the stretched string that gives out musical notes; the slack one is dumb. And if we desire that we may be able to be sure, as our Master was, when He said, 'I know that Thou hearest me always,' we must pray as He did, of whom it is recorded that 'He prayed the more earnestly,' and 'was heard in that He feared.' The word rendered 'the more earnestly' carries in it a metaphor drawn from that very fact that I have referred to. It means 'with the more stretched-out extension and intensity.' If our prayers are to be heard as music in heaven, they must come from a stretched string. Once more, this altar of incense teaches us that kindled prayer delights God. That emblem of the sweet odor is laid hold of with great boldness by more than one Old and New Testament writer, in order to express the marvelous thought that there is a mutual joy in the prayer of faith and love, and that it rises as 'an odor of a sweet smell, a sacrifice acceptable, well pleasing to God.' The cuneiform inscriptions give that thought with characteristic vividness and grossness when they speak about the gods being 'gathered like flies round the steam of the sacrifice.' We have the same thought, freed from all its grossness, when we think that the curling wreaths going up from a heart aspiring and enflamed, come to Him as a sweet odor, and delight His soul.

People say, 'that is anthropomorphism—making God too like a man.' Well, man is like God, at any rate, and surely the teaching of that great name 'Father' carries with it the assurance that just as fathers of flesh are glad when they see that their children like best to be with them, so there is something analogous in that joy before the angels of heaven which the Father has, not only because of the prodigal who comes back, but because of the child who has long been with Him, and is ever seeking to nestle closer to His heart. The Psalmist was lost in wonder and thankfulness that he was able to say 'He was extolled with my tongue.' Surely it should be a gracious, encouraging, strengthening thought to us all, that even our poor aspirations may minister to the divine gladness.

Now let us turn to another thought.

II. This altar shows us where prayer stands in the Christian life.

There are two or three points in regard to its position which it is no fanciful spiritualizing, but simply grasping the underlying meaning of the institution, if we emphasize. First, let me remind you that there was another altar in the outer court, whereon was offered the daily sacrifice for the sins of the people. That altar came first, and the sacrifice had to be offered on it first, before the priest came into the inner court with the coals from that altar, and the incense kindled by them. What does that say to us? The altar of incense is not approached until we have been to the altar of sacrifice. It is no mere arbitrary appointment, nor piece of evangelical narrowness, which says that there is no real access to God, in all the fullness and reality of His revealed character for us sinful men, until our sins have been dealt with, taken away by the Lamb of God, sacrificed for us. And it is simply the transcript of experience which declares that there will be little inclination or desire to come to God with the sacrifice of praise and prayer until we have been to Christ, the sacrifice of propitiation and pardon. Brethren, we need to be cleansed, and we can only be delivered from the unholiness which is the perpetual and necessary barrier to our vision of God by making our very own, through simple faith, the energy and the blessedness of that great Sacrifice of propitiation. Then, and then only, do we properly come to the altar of incense. Its place in the Christian life is second, not first. 'First be reconciled to thy' Father, 'then lay' the incense 'on the altar.'

Again, great and deep lessons are given to us in the place of our altar in regard to the other articles that stood in that inner court. I have said that there were three of them. In the centre this altar of incense; on the one hand the great lamp stand; on the other hand the table with loaves thereon. The one symbolized Israel's function in the world to be its light, which in our function too, and the other with loaves thereon symbolized the consecration to God of Israel's activities, and their results. But between the two, central to both, stood the altar of incense. What does that say as to the place of prayer, defined as I have defined it, in the Christian life? It says this, that the light will burn dim and go out, and the loaves, the expression and the consequences of our activities, will become moldy and dry, unless both are hallowed and sustained by prayer. And that lesson is one which we all need, and which I suppose this generation needs quite as much as, if not more than, any that has gone before it. For life has become so swift and rushing, and from all sides, the Church, the world, society, there come such temptations, and exhortations, and necessities, for strenuous and continuous work, that the basis of all wholesome and vigorous work, communion with God, is but too apt to be put aside and relegated to some inferior position. The carbon points of the electric arc-light are eaten away with tremendous rapidity in the very act of giving forth their illumination, and they need to be continually approximated and to be frequently renewed. The oil is burned away in the act of shining, and the lamp needs to be charged again. If we are to do our work in the world as its lights, and if we are to have any activities fit to be consecrated to God and laid on the Table before the Veil, it can only be by our making the altar of incense the centre, and these others subsidiary.

One last thought—the place of prayer in the Christian life is shadowed for us by the position of this altar in reference to 'the secret place of the Most High,' that mysterious inner court which was dark but for the Shechinah's light, and lonely but for the presence of the worshipping cherubim and the worshipped God. It stood, as we are told a verse or two after my text, 'before the veil.' A straight line drawn from the altar of sacrifice would have bisected the altar of incense as it passed into the mercy-seat and the glory. And that just tells us that the place of prayer in the Christian lift is that it is the direct way of coming close to God. Dear brother, we shall never lift the veil, and stand in 'the secret place of the Most High,' unless we take the altar of incense on our road.

There is one more thought here—

III. The altar of incense shows us how prayer is to be cultivated.

Twice a day, morning and evening, came the officiating priest with his pan of coals and incense, and laid it there; and during all the intervening hours between the morning and the evening the glow lay half hidden in the incense, and there was a faint but continual emission of fragrance from the smoldering mass that had been renewed in the morning, and again in the evening. And does not that say something to us? There must be definite times of distinct prayer if the aroma of devotion is to be diffused through our else scentless days. I ask for no pedantic adherence, with monastic mechanicalness, two hours and times, and forms of petitions. These are needful crutches to many of us. But what I do maintain is that all that talk which we hear so much of in certain quarters nowadays as to its not being necessary for us to have special times of prayer, and as to its being far better to have devotion diffused through our lives, and of how *laborare est orare*—to labour is to pray—all that is pernicious nonsense if it is meant to say that the incense will be fragrant and smolders unless it is stirred up and renewed night and morning. There must be definite times of prayer if there is to be diffused devotion through the day. What would you think of people that said, 'Run your cars by electricity. Get it out of the wires; it will come! Never mind putting up any generating stations'? And not less foolish are they who seek for a devotion permeating life which is not often concentrated into definite and specific acts.

But the other side is as true. It is bad to clot your religion into lumps, and to leave the rest of the life without it. There must be the smoldering all day long. 'Rejoice evermore; pray without ceasing.' You can pray thus. Not set prayer, of course; but a reference to Him, a thought of Him, like some sweet melody, 'so sweet we know not we are listening to it,' may breathe its fragrance, and diffuse its warmth into the commonest and smallest of our daily activities. It was when Gideon was threshing wheat that the angel appeared to him. It was when Elisha was plowing that the divine inspiration touched him. It was when the disciples were fishing that they saw the Form on the shore. And when we are in the way of our common life it is possible that the Lord may meet us, and that our souls may be aspiring to Him. Then work will be worship; then burdens will be lightened; then our lamps will burn; then the fruits of our daily lives will ripen; then our lives will be noble; then our spirits will rest as well as soar, and find fruition and aspiration perpetually alternating in stable succession of eternal progress.

RANSOM FOR SOULS

'Then shall they give every man a ransom for his soul.' —Exodus 30:12.

This remarkable provision had a religious intention. Connect it with the tax-money which Peter found in the fish's mouth.

I. Its meaning. Try to realize an Israelite's thoughts at the census. 'I am enrolled among the people and army of God: am I worthy? What am I, to serve so holy a God?' The payment was meant—

> *(a)* To excite the sense of sin. This should be present in all approach to God, in all service; accompanying the recognition of our Christian standing. Our sense of sin is far too slight and weak; this defect is at the root of much feebleness in popular religion. The sense of sin must embrace not outward acts only, but inner spirit also.

> *(b)* To suggest the possibility of expiation. It was 'ransom' *i.e.* 'covering,' something paid that guilt might be taken away and sin regarded as non-existent. This is, of course, obviously, only a symbol. No tax could satisfy God for sin. The very smallness of the amount shows that it is symbolical only. 'Not with corruptible things as silver' is man redeemed.

II. Its identity for all. Rich or poor, high or low, all men are equal in sin. There are surface differences and degrees, but a deep identity beneath. So on the same principle all souls are of the same value. Here is the true democracy of Christianity. So there is one ransom for all, for the need of all is identical.

III. Its use. It was melted down for use in the sanctuary, so as to be a 'memorial' permanently present to God when His people met with Him. The greater portion was made into bases for the boards of the sanctuary. That is, God's dwelling with men and our communion with Him all rest on the basis of ransom. We are 'brought nigh by the blood of Christ.'

'The rich shall not give more, and the poor shall not give less than half a shekel....'—Exodus 30:15.

This tax was exacted on numbering the people. It was a very small amount, about fifteen pence, so it was clearly symbolical in its significance. Notice—

I. The broad principle of equality of all souls in the sight of God. Contrast the reign of caste and class in heathendom with the democracy of Judaism and of Christianity.

II. The universal sinfulness. Payment of the tax was a confession that all were alike in this: not that all were equally sinful, but all were sinful, whatever variations of degree might exist.

'There is no difference, for all have sinned and come short of the glory of God.'

III. The one ransom. It was a prophecy of which *we* know the meaning. Recall the incident of the 'stator' in the fish's mouth.

Christ declares His exemption from the tax. Yet He voluntarily comes under it, and He provides the payment of it for Himself and for Peter.

He does so by a miracle.

The Apostle has to 'take and give it'; so faith is called into exercise.

Thus there is but one Sacrifice for all; and the poorest can exercise faith and the richest can do no more. 'None other name.'

THE GOLDEN CALF

'And when the people saw that Moses delayed to come down out of the mount, the people gathered themselves together unto Aaron, and said unto him, Up, make us gods, which shall go before us; for as for this Moses, the man that brought us up out of the land of Egypt, we know not what is become of him.

2. And Aaron said unto them, Break off the golden earrings, which are in the ears of your wives, of your sons, and of your daughters, and bring them unto me.

3. And all the people brake off the golden earrings which were in their ears, and brought them unto Aaron.

4. And he received them at their hand, and fashioned it with a graving-tool, after he had made it a molten calf: and they said, These be thy gods, O Israel, which brought thee up out of the land of Egypt.

5. And when Aaron saw it, he built an altar before it; and Aaron made proclamation, and said, To-morrow is a feast to the Lord.

6. And they rose up early on the morrow, and offered burnt offerings, and brought peace offerings; and the people sat down to eat and to drink, and rose up to play.

7. And the Lord said unto Moses, Go, get thee down; for thy people, which thou broughtest out of the land of Egypt, have corrupted themselves:

8. They have turned aside quickly out of the way which I commanded them: they have made them a molten calf, and have worshipped it, and have sacrificed thereunto, and said, These be thy gods, O Israel, which have brought thee up out of the land of Egypt....

And it came to pass on the morrow, that Moses said unto the people, Ye have sinned a great sin: and now I will go up unto the Lord; peradventure I shall make an atonement for your sin. And Moses returned unto the Lord, and said, Oh! this people have sinned a great sin, and have made them gods of gold. Yet now, if Thou wilt forgive their sin—; and if not, blot me, I pray thee, out of Thy book which Thou hast written. And the Lord said unto Moses, Whosoever hath sinned against Me, him will I blot out of My book. Therefore now go, lead the people unto the place of which I have spoken unto thee. Behold, Mine Angel shall go before thee: nevertheless in the day when I visit I will visit their sin upon them. And the Lord plagued the people, because they made the calf, which Aaron made.'—Exodus 32:1-8; .

It was not yet six weeks since the people had sworn, 'All that the Lord hath spoken will we do, and be obedient.' The blood of the covenant, sprinkled on them, was scarcely dry when they flung off allegiance to Jehovah. Such short-lived loyalty to Him can never have been genuine. That mob of slaves was galvanized by Moses into obedience; and since their acceptance of Jehovah was in reality only yielding to the power of one strong will and its earnest faith, of course it collapsed as soon as Moses disappeared. We have to note, first, the people's universal revolt. The language of verse 1 may easily hide to a careless reader the gravity and unanimity of the apostasy. 'The people gathered themselves together.' It was a national rebellion, a flood which swept away even some faithful, timid hearts. No voices ventured to protest. What were the elders, who shortly before 'saw the God of Israel,' doing to be passive at such a crisis? Was there no one to bid the fickle multitude look up to the summit overhead, where the red flames glowed, or to remind them of the hosts of Egypt lying stark and dead on the shore? Was Miriam cowed too, and her song forgotten?

We need not cast stones at these people; for we also have short memories for either the terrible or the gracious revelations of God in our own lives. But we may learn the lesson that God's lovers have to set themselves sometimes dead against the rush of popular feeling, and that there are times when silence or compliance is sin. It would have been easy for the rebels to have ignored Aaron, and made gods for themselves. But they desired to involve him in their apostasy, and to get 'official sanction' for it. He had been left by Moses as his lieutenant, and so to get him implicated was to stamp the movement as a regular and entire revolt. The demand 'to make gods' (or, more probably, 'a god') flew in the face of both the first and second commandments. For Jehovah, who had forbidden the forming of any image, was denied in the act of making it. To disobey Him was to cast Him off. The ground of the rebellion was the craving for a visible object of trust and a visible guide, as is seen by the reason assigned for the demand for an image. Moses was out of sight; they must have something to look at as their leader. Moses had disappeared, and, to these people who had only been heaved up to the height of believing in Jehovah by Moses, Jehovah had disappeared with him. They sank down again to the level of other races as soon as that strong lever ceased to lift their heavy apprehensions.

How ridiculous the assertion that they did not know what had become of Moses! They knew that he was up there with Jehovah. The elders could have told them that. The fire on the mount might have burned in on all minds the confirmation. Note, too, the black ingratitude and plain denial of Jehovah in 'the *man* that brought us up out of the land of Egypt.' They refuse to recognize God's part. It was Moses only who had done it; and now that he is gone they must have a visible god, like other nations. Still sadder than their sense-bound wish is Aaron's compliance. He knew as well as we do what he should have said, but, like many another man in influential position, when beset by popular cries, he was frightened, and yielded when he should have 'set his face like a flint.' His compliance has in essentials been often repeated, especially by priests and ministers of religion who have lent their superior abilities or opportunities to carry out the wishes of the ignorant populace, and debased religion or watered down its prohibitions, to please and retain hold of them. The Church has incorporated much from heathenism. Roman Catholic missionaries have permitted 'converts' to keep their old usages. Protestant teachers have acquiesced in, and been content to find the brains to carry out, compromises between sense and soul, God's commands and men's inclinations. We need not discuss the metallurgy of verse 4. But clearly Aaron asked for the earrings, not, as some would have it, hoping that vanity and covetousness would hinder their being given, but simply in order to get gold for the bad work which he was ready to do. The reason for making the thing in the shape of a calf is probably the Egyptian worship of Apis in that form, which would be familiar to the people.

We must note that it was the people who said, 'These be thy gods, O Israel!' Aaron seems to keep in the rear, as it were. He makes the calf, and hands it over, and leaves them to hail it and worship. Like all cowards, he thought that he was lessening his guilt by thus keeping in the background. Feeble natures are fond of such subterfuges, and deceive themselves by them; but they do not shift their sin off their shoulders. Then he comes in again with an impotent attempt to diminish the gravity of the revolt. 'When he *saw* this,' he tried to turn the flood into another channel, and so proclaimed a 'feast to Jehovah'!—as if He could be worshipped by flagrant defiance of His commandments, or as if He had not been disavowed by the ascription to the calf, made that morning out of their own trinkets, of the deliverance from Egypt. A poor, inconsequential attempt to save appearances and hallow sin by writing God's name on it! The 'god' whom the Israelites worshipped under the image of a calf, was no less another 'god before Me,' though it was called by the name of Jehovah. If the people had their idol, it mattered nothing to them, and it mattered as little to Jehovah, what 'name' it bore. The wild orgies of the morrow were not the worship which He accepts.

What a contrast between the plain and the mountain! Below, the shameful feast, with its parody of sacrifice and its sequel of lust-inflamed dancing; above, the awful colloquy between the all-seeing righteous Judge and the intercessor! The people had cast off Jehovah, and Jehovah no more calls them 'My,' but '*thy* people.' They had ascribed their Exodus first to Moses, and next to the calf. Jehovah speaks of it as the work of Moses. A terrible separation of Himself from them lies in '*thy* people, which *thou* broughtest up,' and Moses' bold rejoinder emphasizes the relation and act which Jehovah seems to suppress (verse 11). Observe that the divine voice refuses to give any weight to Aaron's trick of compromise. These are no worshippers of Jehovah who are howling and dancing below there. They are 'worshipping *it*, and sacrificing to it,' not to Him. The cloaks of sin may partly cover its ugliness here, but they are transparent to His eyes, and many a piece of worship, which is said to be directed to Him, is, in His sight, rank idolatry.

We do not deal with the magnificent courage of Moses, his single-handed arresting of the wild rebellion, and the severe punishment by which he trampled out the fire. But we must keep his severity in mind if we would rightly judge his self-sacrificing devotion, and his self-sacrificing devotion if we would rightly judge his severity. No words of ours can make more sublime his utter self-abandonment for the sake of the people among whom he had just been flaming in wrath, and smiting like a destroying angel. That was a great soul which had for its poles such justice and such love. The very words of his prayer, in their abruptness, witness to his deep emotion. 'If Thou wilt forgive their sin' stands as an incomplete sentence, left incomplete because the speaker is so profoundly moved. Sometimes broken words are the best witnesses of our earnestness. The alternative clause reaches the high-water mark of passionate love, ready to give up everything for the sake of its objects. The 'book of life' is often spoken of in Scripture, and it is an interesting study to bring together the places where the idea occurs (see Psalm 69:28; Daniel 12:1; Philippians 4:3; Revelation 3:5). The allusion is to the citizens' roll (Psalm 87:6).

Those whose names are written there have the privileges of citizenship, and, as it is the 'book of life' (or '*of the living*'), life in the widest sense is secured to them. To blot out of it, therefore, is to cut a man off from fellowship in the city of God, and from participation in life. Moses was so absorbed in his vocation that his life was less to him than the well-being of Israel. How far he saw into the darkness beyond the grave we cannot say; but, at least, he was content, and desirous to die on earth, if thereby Israel might continue to be God's people. And probably he had some gleam of light beyond, which enhanced the greatness of his offered sacrifice. To die, whatever loss of communion with God that involved here or hereafter, would be sweet if thereby he could purchase Israel's restoration to God's favour. We cannot but think of Paul willing to be separated from Christ for his brethren's sake. We may well think of a greater than Moses or Paul, who did bear the loss which they were willing to bear, and died that sin might be forgiven. Moses was a true type of Christ in that act of supreme self-sacrifice; and all the heroism, the identification of himself with his people, the love which willingly accepts death, that makes his prayer one of the greatest deeds on the page of history, are repeated in infinitely sweeter, more heart-subduing fashion in the story of the Cross. Let us not omit duly to honour the servant; let us not neglect to honour and love infinitely more the Lord. 'This man was counted worthy of more glory than Moses.' Let us see that we render Him

THE SWIFT DECAY OF LOVE

'And Moses turned, and went down from the mount, and the two tables of the testimony were in his hand: the tables were written on both their sides; on the one side and on the other were they written. And the tables were the work of God, and the writing was the writing of God, graven upon the tables. And when Joshua heard the noise of the people as they shouted, he said unto Moses, There is a noise of war in the camp. And he said, It is not the voice of them that shout for mastery, neither is it the voice of them that cry for being overcome: but the noise of them that sing do I hear. And it came to pass, as soon as he came nigh unto the camp, that he saw the calf, and the dancing: and Moses' anger waxed hot, and he cast the tables out of his hands, and brake them beneath the mount. And he took the calf which they had made, and burnt it in the fire, and ground it to powder, and strewed it upon the water, and made the children of Israel drink of it. And Moses said unto Aaron, What did this people unto thee, that thou hast brought so great a sin upon them? And Aaron said, Let not the anger of my lord wax hot: thou knowest the people, that they are set on mischief.

For they said unto me, Make us gods, which shall go before us: for as for this Moses, the man that brought us up out of the land of Egypt, we know not what is become of him. And I said unto them, Whosoever hath any gold, let them break it off. So they gave it me: then I cast it into the fire, and there came out this calf. And when Moses saw that the people were naked; (for Aaron had made them naked unto their shame among their enemies:) Then Moses stood in the gate of the camp, and said, Who is on the Lord's side? let him come unto me. And all the sons of Levi gathered themselves together unto him.'—Exodus 32:15-26.

Moses and Joshua are on their way down from the mountain, the former carrying the tables in his hands and a heavier burden in his heart,—the thought of the people's swift apostasy. Joshua's soldierly ear interprets the shouts which are borne up to them as war-cries; 'He snuffeth the battle afar off, and saith Aha!' But Moses knew that they meant worse than war, and his knowledge helped his ear to distinguish a cadence and unison in the noise, unlike the confused mingling of the victors' yell of triumph and the shriek of the conquered. If we were dealing with fiction, we should admire the masterly dramatic instinct which lets the ear anticipate the eye, and so prepares us for the hideous sight that burst on these two at some turn in the rocky descent.

I. Note, then, what they saw. The vivid story puts it all in two words,—'the calf and the dancing.' There in the midst, perhaps on some pedestal, was the shameful copy of the Egyptian Apis; and whirling round it in mad circles, working themselves into frenzy by rapid motion and frantic shouts, were the people,—men and women, mingled in the licentious dance, who, six short weeks before, had sworn to the Covenant. Their bestial deity in the centre, and they compassing it with wild hymns, were a frightful contradiction of that grey altar and the twelve encircling stones which they had so lately reared, and which stood unregarded, a bowshot off, as a silent witness against them. Note the strange, irresistible fascination of idolatry. Clearly the personal influence of Moses was the only barrier against it.

The people thought that he had disappeared, and, if so, Jehovah had disappeared with him. We wonder at their relapses into idolatry, but we forget that it was then universal, that Israel was at the beginning of its long training, that not even a divine revelation could produce harvest in seedtime, and that to look for a final and complete deliverance from the 'veil that was spread over all nations,' at this stage, is like expecting a newly reclaimed bit of the backwoods to grow grass as thick and velvety as has carpeted some lawn that has been mown and cared for a century. Grave condemnation is the due of these short-memorized rebels, who set up their 'abomination' in sight of the fire on Sinai; but that should not prevent our recognizing the evidence which their sin affords of the tremendous power of idolatry in that stage of the world's history. Israel's proneness to fall back to heathenism makes it certain that a supernatural revelation is needed to account for their possession of the loftier faith which was so far above them.

That howling, leaping crowd tells what sort of religion they would have 'evolved' if left to themselves. Where did 'Thou shalt have none other gods beside Me' come from? Note the confusion of thought, so difficult for us to understand, which characterizes idolatry. What a hopelessly inconsequential cry that was, 'Make us gods, which shall go before us!' and what a muddle of contradictions it was that men should say 'These be thy gods,' though they knew that the thing was made yesterday out of their own earrings! It took more than a thousand years to teach the nation the force of the very self-evident argument, as it seems to us, 'the workman made it, therefore it is not God.' The theory that the idol is only a symbol is not the actual belief of idolaters. It is a product of the study, but the worshipper unites in his thought the irreconcilable beliefs that it was made and is divine. A goldsmith will make and sell a Madonna, and when it is put in the cathedral, will kneel before it. Note what was the sin here. It is generally taken for granted that it was a breach of the second, not of the first, commandment, and Aaron's proclamation of 'a feast to the Lord' is taken as proving this. Aaron was probably trying to make an impossible compromise, and to find some salve for his conscience; but it does not follow that the people accepted the half-and-half suggestion. Leaders who try to control a movement which they disapprove, by seeming to accept it, play a dangerous game, and usually fail. But whether the people call the calf 'Jehovah' or 'Apis' matters very little. There would be as complete apostasy to another god, though the other god was called by the same name, if all that really makes his 'name' was left out, and foreign elements were brought in. Such worship as these wild dances, offered to an image, broke both the commandments, no matter by what name the image was invoked. The roots of idolatry are in all men. The gross form of it is impossible to us; but the need for aid from sense, the dependence on art for wings to our devotion, which is a growing danger to-day, is only the modern form of the same dislike of a purely spiritual religion which sent these people dancing round their calf.

II. Mark Moses' blaze of wrath and courageous, prompt action. He dashes the tables on the rock, as if to break the record of the useless laws which the people have already broken, and, with his hands free, flings himself without pause into the midst of the excited mob. Verses 19 and 20 bear the impression of his rapid, decisive action in their succession of clauses, each tacked on to the preceding by a simple 'and.' Stroke followed stroke. His fiery earnestness swept over all obstacles, the base riot ceased, the ashamed dancers slunk away. Some true hearts would gather about him, and carry out his commands; but he did the real work, and, single-handed, cowed and controlled the mob. No doubt, it took more time than the brief narrative, at first sight, would suggest. The image is flung into the fire from which it had come out. The fire made it, and the fire shall unmake it. We need not find difficulty in 'burning' a golden idol. That does not mean 'calcined,' and the writer is not guilty of a blunder, nor needed to be taught that you cannot burn gold. The next clause says that after it was 'burned,' it was still solid; so that, plainly, all that is meant is, that the metal was reduced to a shapeless lump. That would take some time. Then it was broken small; there were plenty of rocks to grind it up on. That would take some more time, but not a finger was lifted to prevent it. Then the more or less finely broken up fragments are flung into the brook, and, with grim irony, the people are bid to drink. 'You shall have enough of your idol, since you love him so. Here, down with him! You will have to take the consequences of your sin. You must drink as you have brewed.' It is at once a contemptuous demonstration of the idol's impotence, and a picture of the sure retribution.

But we may learn two things from this figure of the indignant lawgiver. One is, that the temper in which to regard idolatry is not one of equable indifference nor of scientific investigation, but that some heat of moral indignation is wholesome. We are all studying comparative mythology now, and getting much good from it; but we are in some danger of forgetting that these strange ideas and practices, which we examine at our ease, have spread spiritual darkness and moral infection over continents and through generations. Let us understand them, by all means; let us be thankful to find fragments of truth in, or innocent origins of, repulsive legends; but do not let the student swallow up the Christian in us, nor our minds lose their capacity of wholesome indignation at the systems, blended with Christ-like pity and effort for the victims. We may learn, further, how strong a man is when he is all aflame with true zeal for God. The suddenness of Moses' reappearance, the very audacity of his act, the people's habit of obedience, all helped to carry him through the crisis; but the true secret of his swift victory was his own self-forgetting faith. There is contagion in pure religious enthusiasm. It is the strongest of all forces. One man, with God at his back, is always in the majority. He whose whole soul glows with the pure fire, will move among men like flame in stubble. 'All things are possible to him that believeth.' Consecrated daring, animated by love and fed with truth, is all-conquering.

III. Note the weaker nature of Aaron, taking refuge in a transparent lie. Probably his dialogue with his brother came in before the process described in the former verses was accomplished. But the narrative keeps all that referred to the destruction of the idol together, and goes by subject rather than by time. We do not learn how Moses had come to know Aaron's share in the sin, but his question is one of astonishment. Had they bewitched him anyhow? or what inducement had led him so far astray? The stronger and devoted soul cannot conceive how the weaker had yielded. Aaron's answer puts the people's wish forward. 'They said, Make us gods'; that was all which they had 'done.' A poor excuse, as Aaron feels even while he is stammering it out. What would Moses have answered if the people had 'said' so to him? Did he, standing there, with the heat of his struggle on him yet, look like a man that would acknowledge any demand of a mob as a reason for a ruler's compliance? It is the coward's plea. How many ecclesiastics and statesmen since then have had no better to offer for their acts! Such fear of the Lord as shriveled before the breath of popular clamor could have had no deep roots. One of the first things to learn, whether we are in prominent or in private positions, is to hold by our religious convictions in supreme indifference to all surrounding voices, and to let no threats nor entreaties lead us to take one step beyond or against conscience.

Aaron feels the insufficiency of the plea, when he has to put it into plain words to such a listener, and so he flies to the resource of timid and weak natures, a lie. For what did he ask the gold, and put it into the furnace, unless he meant to make a god? Perhaps he had told the people the same story, as priests in all lands have been apt to claim a miraculous origin for idols. And he repeats it now, as if, were it true, he would plead the miracle as a vindication of the worship as well as his absolution. But the lie is too transparent to deserve even an answer, and Moses turns silently from him. Aaron's was evidently the inferior nature, and was less deeply stamped with the print of heaven than his brother's. His feeble compliance is recorded as a beacon for all persons in places of influence or authority, warning them against self-interested or cowardly yielding to a popular demand, at the sacrifice of the purity of truth and the approval of their own consciences. He was not the last priest who has allowed the supposed wishes of the populace to shape his representations of God, and has knowingly dropped the standard of duty or sullied the clear brightness of truth in deference to the many-voiced monster.

IV. Note the rallying of true hearts round Moses. The Revised Version reads 'broken loose' instead of 'naked,' and the correction is valuable. It explains the necessity for the separation of those who yet remained bound by the restraints of God's law, and for the terrible retribution that followed. The rebellion had not been stamped out by the destruction of the calf; and though Moses' dash into their midst had cowed the rebels for a time, things had gone too far to settle down again at once. The camp was in insurrection. It was more than a riot, it was a revolution. With the rapid eye of genius, Moses sees the gravity of the crisis, and, with equally swift decisiveness, acts so as to meet it. He 'stood in the gate of the camp,' and made the nucleus for the still faithful. His summons puts the full seriousness of the moment clearly before the people. They have come to a fork in the road. They must be either for Jehovah or against Him. There can be no mixing up of the worship of Jehovah and the images of Egypt, no tampering with God's service in obedience to popular clamor. It must be one thing or other. This is no time for the family of 'Mr. Facing-both-ways'; the question for each man is, 'Under which King?' Moses' unhesitating confidence that he is God's soldier, and that to be at his side is to be on God's side, was warranted in him, but has often been repeated with less reason by eager contenders, as they believed themselves to be, for God. No doubt, it becomes us to be modest and cautious in calling all true friends of God to rank themselves with us. But where the issue is between foul wrong and plain right, between palpable idolatry, error, or unbridled lust, and truth, purity, and righteousness, the Christian combatant for these is entitled to send round the fiery cross, and proclaim a crusade in God's name. There will always be plenty of people with cold water to pour on enthusiasm. We should be all the better for a few more, who would venture to feel that they are fighting for God, and to summon all who love Him to come to their and His help. Moses' own tribe responded to the summons. And, no doubt, Aaron was there too, galvanized into a nobler self by the courage and fervor of his brother, and, let us hope, urged by penitence, to efface the memory of his faithlessness by his heroism now.

We do not go on to the dreadful retribution, which must be regarded, not as massacre, but as legal execution. It is folly to apply to it, or to other analogous instances, the ideas of this Christian century. We need not be afraid to admit that there has been a development of morality. The retributions of a stern age were necessarily stern. But if we want to understand the heart of Moses, or of Moses' God, we must not look only at the ruler of a wild people trampling out a revolt at the sacrifice of many lives, but listen to him, as the next section of the narrative shows him, pleading with tears for the rebels, and offering even to let his own name be blotted out of God's book if their sin might be forgiven. So, coupling the two parts of his conduct together, we may learn a little more clearly a lesson, of which this age has much need,—the harmony of retributive justice and pitying love; and may come to understand that Moses learned both the one and the other by fellowship with the God in whom they both dwell in perfection and concord.

THE MEDIATOR'S THREEFOLD PRAYER

'And Moses said unto the Lord, See, Thou sayest unto me, Bring up this people: and Thou hast not let me know whom Thou wilt send with me. Yet Thou hast said, I know thee by name, and thou hast also found grace in My sight.. Now therefore, I pray Thee, if I have found grace in Thy sight, show me now Thy way, that I may know Thee, that I may find grace in Thy sight: and consider that this nation is Thy people. And He said, My presence shall go with thee, and I will give thee rest. And he said unto Him, If Thy presence go not with me, carry us not up hence. For wherein shall it be known here that I and Thy people have found grace in Thy sight? Is it not in that Thou goest with us! So shall we be separated, I and Thy people, from all the people that are upon the face of the earth, And the Lord said unto Moses, I will do this thing also that thou hast spoken: for thou hast found grace in My sight, and I know thee by name. And he said, I beseech Thee, show me Thy glory. And He said, I will make all My goodness pass before thee, and I will proclaim the name of the Lord before thee; and will be gracious to whom I will be gracious, and will shew mercy on whom I will shew mercy. And he said, Thou canst not see My face: for there shall no man see Me, and live. And the Lord said, Behold, there is a place by Me, and thou shalt stand upon a rock: And it shall come to pass, while My glory passeth by, that I will put thee in a cleft of the rock, and will cover thee with My hand while I pass by: And I will take away Mine hand, and thou shall see My back parts; but My face shall not be seen.'—Exodus 33:12-23.

The calf worship broke the bond between God and Israel. Instead of His presence, 'an angel' is to lead them, for His presence could only be destruction. Mourning spreads through the camp, in token of which all ornaments are laid aside. The fate of the nation is in suspense, and the people wait, in sad attire, till God knows 'what to do unto' them. The Tabernacle is carried beyond the precincts of the camp, in witness of the breach, and all the future is doubtful. The preceding context describes (vs.7-11) not one event, but the standing order of these dark days, when the camp had to be left if God was to be found, and when Moses alone received tokens of God's friendship, and the people stood wistfully and tremblingly gazing from afar, while the cloudy pillar wavered down to the Tabernacle door. Duty brought Moses back from such communion; but Joshua did not need to come near the tents of the evil-doers, and, in the constancy of devout desire, made his home in the Tabernacle. In one of these interviews, so close and familiar, the wonderful dialogue here recorded occurred. It turns round three petitions, to each of which the Lord answers.

I. We have the leader's prayer for himself, with the over-abundant answer of God. In the former chapter, we had the very sublimity of intercession, in which the stern avenger of idolatry poured out his self-sacrificing love for the stiff-necked nation whom he had had to smite, and offered himself a victim for them. Here his first prayer is mainly for himself, but it is not therefore a selfish prayer. Rather he prays for gifts to himself, to fit him for his service to them. We may note separately the prayer, and the pleas on which it is urged. 'Show me now Thy way (or ways), that I may know Thee.' The desire immediately refers to the then condition of things. As we have pointed out, it was a time of suspense. In the strong metaphor of the context, God was making up His mind on His course, and

Israel was waiting with hushed breath for the *denouement*. It was not the entrance of the nation into the promised land which was in doubt, but the manner of their guidance, and the penalties of their idolatry. These things Moses asked to know, and especially, as verse 12 shows, to receive some more definite communication as to their leader than the vague 'an angel.' But the specific knowledge of God's 'way' was yearned for by him, mainly, as leading on to a deeper and fuller and more blessed knowledge of God Himself, and that again as leading to a fuller possession of God's favour, which, as already in some measure possessed, lay at the foundation of the whole prayer. The connection of thought here goes far beyond the mere immediate blessing, which Moses needed at the moment. That cry for insight into the purposes and methods of Him whom the soul trusts, amid darkness and suspense, is the true voice of sonship. The more deeply it sees into these, the more does the devout soul feel the contrast between the spot of light in which it lives and the encircling obscurity, and the more does it yearn for the further setting back of the boundaries. Prayer does more than effort, for satisfying that desire. Nor is it mere curiosity or the desire for intellectual clearness that moves the longing. For the end of knowing God's ways is, for the devout man, a deeper, more blessed knowledge of God Himself, who is best known in His deeds; and the highest, most blessed issue of the God-given knowledge of God, is the conscious sunshine of His favour shining ever on His servant. That is not a selfish religion which, beginning with the assurance that we have found grace in His sight, seeks to climb, by happy paths of growing knowledge of Him as manifested in His ways, to a consciousness of that favour which is made stable and profound by clear insight into the depths of His purposes and acts.

The pleas on which this prayer is urged are two: the suppliant's heavy tasks, and God's great assurances to him. He boldly reminds God of what He has set him to do, and claims that he should be furnished with what is needful for discharging his commission. How can he lead if he is kept in the dark? When we are as sure as Moses was of God's charge to us, we may be as bold as he in asking the needful equipment for it. God does not send His servants out to sow without seed, or to fight without a sword. His command is His pledge. He smiles approval when His servants' confidence assumes even bold forms, which sound like remonstrance and a suspicion that He was forgetting, for He discerns the underlying eagerness to do His will, and the trust in Him. The second plea is built on God's assurances of intimate and distinguishing knowledge and favour. He had said that He knew Moses 'by name,' by all these calls and familiar interviews which gave him the certainty of his individual relation to, and his special appointment from, the Lord. Such prerogative was inconsistent with reserve. The test of friendship is confidence. So pleads Moses, and God recognizes the plea. 'I call you not servants; for the servant knoweth not what his lord doeth; but I have called you friends; for all things that I have heard of my Father I have made known unto you.' The plea based upon the relation of the people to God is subordinate in this first prayer. It is thrown in at the end almost as an afterthought; it boldly casts responsibility off Moses on to God, and does so to enforce the prayer that he should be equipped with all requisites for his work, as if he had said, 'It is more Thy concern than mine, that I should be able to lead them.' The divine answer is a promise to go not with the people, but with Moses. It is therefore not yet a full resolving of the doubtful matter, nor directly a reply to Moses' prayer. In one aspect it is less, and in another more, than had been asked. It seals to the man and to the leader the assurance that for himself he shall have the continual presence of God, in his soul and in his work, and that, in all the weary march, he will have rest, and will come to a fuller rest at its end. Thus God ever answers the true hearts that seek to know Him, and to be fitted for their tasks. Whether the precise form of desire be fulfilled or no, the issue of such bold and trustful pleading is always the inward certainty of God's face shining on us, and the experience of repose, deep and untroubled in the midst of toil, so that we may be at once pilgrims towards, and dwellers in, 'the house of the Lord,'

II. We have the intercessor's prayer for the people, with the answer (vs.15-17). If the promise of verse 14 is taken as referring to the people, there is nothing additional asked in this second stage, and the words of verse 17, 'this thing also,' are inexplicable. Observe that 'with me' in verse 15 is a supplement, and that the 'us' of the next clause, as well as the whole cast of verse 16, suggests that we should rather supply 'with us,' The substance, then, of the second petition, is the extension of the promise, already given to Moses for himself, to the entire nation. Observe how he identifies himself with them, making them 'partakers' in his grace, and reiterating 'I and Thy people,' as if he would have no blessing which was not shared by them. He seeks that the withdrawal of God's presence, which had been the consequence of Israel's withdrawal from God, should be reversed, and that not he alone, but all the rebels, might still possess His presence.

    The plea for this prayer is God's honour, which was concerned in making it plain even in the remote wilderness, to the wandering tribes there, that His hand was upon Israel. Moses expands the argument which he had just touched before. The thought of His own glory as the motive of God's acts, may easily be so put at to be repulsive; but at bottom it is the same as to say that His motive is love—for the glory which He seeks is the communication of true thoughts concerning His character, that men may be made glad and like Himself thereby. Moses has learned that God's heart must long to reveal its depth of mercy, and therefore he pleads that even sinful Israel should not be left by God, in order that some light from His face may strike into a dark world. There is wide benevolence, as well as deep insight into the desires of God, in the plea. The divine answer yields unconditionally to the request, and rests the reason for so doing wholly on the relation between God and Moses. The plea which he had urged in lowly boldness as the foundation of both his prayers is endorsed, and, for his sake, the divine presence is again granted to the people.

Can we look at this scene without seeing in it the operation on a lower field of the same great principle of intercession, which reaches its unique example in Jesus Christ? It is not arbitrary forcing of the gospel into the history, but simply the recognition of the essence of the history, when we see in it a foreshadowing of our great High-priest. He, too, knits Himself so closely with us, both by the assumption of our manhood and by the identity of loving sympathy, that He accepts nothing from the Father's hand for Himself alone. He, too, presents Himself before God, and says 'I and Thy people.' The great seal of proof for the world that He is the beloved of God, lies in the divine guardianship and guidance of His servants. His prayer for them prevails, and the reason for its prevalence is God's delight in Him. The very sublime of self- sacrificing love was in the lawgiver, but the height of his love, measured against the immeasurable altitude of Christ's, is as a mole-hill to the Andes.

III. We have the last soaring desire which rises above the limits of the present. These three petitions teach the insatiableness, if we may use the word, of devout desires. Each request granted brings on a greater. 'The gift doth stretch itself as 'tis received.' Enjoyment increases capacity, an increase of capacity is increase of desire. God being infinite, and man capable of indefinite growth, neither the widening capacity nor the infinite supply can have limits. This is not the least of the blessings of a devout life, that the appetite grows with what it feeds on, and that, while there is always satisfaction, there is never satiety.

Moses' prayer sounds presumptuous, but it was heard unblamed, and granted in so far as possible. It was a venial error—if error it may be called—that a soul, touched with the flame of divine love, should aspire beyond the possibilities of mortality. At all events, it was a fault in which he has had few imitators. *Our* desires keep but too well within the limits of the possible. The precise meaning of the petition must be left undetermined. Only this is clear, that it was something far beyond even that face-to-face intercourse which he had had, as well as beyond that vision granted to the elders. If we are to take 'glory' in its usual sense, it would mean the material symbol of God's presence, which shone at the heart of the pillar, and dwelt afterwards between the cherubim, but probably we must attach a loftier meaning to it here, and rather think of what we should call the uncreated and infinite divine essence. Only do not let us make Moses talk like a metaphysician or a theological professor. Rather we should hear in his cry the voice of a soul thrilled through and through with the astounding consciousness of God's favour, blessed with love-gifts in answered prayers, and yearning for more of that light which it feels to be life.

And if the petition be dark, the answer is yet more obscure 'with excess of light.' Mark how it begins with granting, not with refusing. It tells how much the loving desire has power to bring, before it speaks of what in it must be denied. There is infinite tenderness in that order of response. It speaks of a heart that does not love to say 'no,' and grants our wishes up to the very edge of the possible, and wraps the bitterness of any refusal in the sweet envelope of granted requests. A broad distinction is drawn between that in God which can be revealed, and that which cannot. The one is 'glory,' the other 'goodness,' corresponding, we might almost say, to the distinction between the 'moral' and the 'natural' attributes of God. But, whatever mysterious revelation under the guise of vision may be concealed in these words, and in the fulfillment of them in the next chapter, they belong to the 'things which it is impossible for a man to utter,' even if he has received them. We are on more intelligible ground in the next clause of the promise, the proclamation of 'the Name.' That expression is, in Scripture, always used as meaning the manifested character of God. It is a revelation addressed to the spirit, not to the sense. It is the translation, so far as it is capable of translation, of the vision which it accompanied; it is the treasure which Moses bore away from Sinai, and has shared among us all. The reason for his prayer was probably his desire to have his mediatorial office confirmed and perfected; and it was so, by that proclamation of the Name. The reason for this marvelous gift is next set forth as being God's own unconditional grace and mercy. He is His own motive, His own reason. Just as the independent and absolute fullness of His being is expressed by the name 'I am that I am,' so the independent and absolute freeness of His mercy, whether in granting Moses' prayer or in pardoning the people, is expressed by 'I will shew mercy on whom I will shew mercy.' Not till all this exuberance of gracious answer has smoothed the way does the denial of the impossible request come; and even then it is so worded as to lay all the emphasis on what is granted, and to show that the refusal is but another phase of love. The impossibility of beholding the Face is reiterated, and then the careful provisions which God will make for the fulfillment of the possible part of the bold wish are minutely detailed. The distinction between the revealable and unrevealable, which has been already expressed by the contrast of 'glory' and 'grace,' now appears in the distinction between the 'face' which cannot be looked on, and the 'back' which may be.

Human language and thought are out of their depth here. We must be content to see a dim splendor shining through the cloudy words, to know that there was granted to one man a realization of God's presence, and a revelation of His character, so far transcending ordinary experiences as that it was fitly called sight, but yet as far beneath the glory of His being as the comparatively imperfect knowledge of a man's form, when seen only from behind, is beneath that derived from looking him in the face. But whatever was the singular prerogative of the lawgiver, as he gazed from the cleft of the rock at the receding glory, we see more than he ever did; and the Christian child, who looks upon the 'glory of God in the face of Jesus Christ,' has a vision which outshines the flashing radiance that shone round Moses. It deepened his convictions, confirmed his faith, added to his assurance of his divine commission, but only added to his knowledge of God by the proclamation of the Name, and that Name is more fully proclaimed in our ears. Sinai, with all its thunders, is silent before Calvary. And he who has Jesus Christ to declare God's Name to him need not envy the lawgiver on the mountain, nor even the saints in heaven.

GOD PROCLAIMING HIS OWN NAME

'The Lord passed by before him, and proclaimed, The Lord, the Lord God, merciful and gracious, longsuffering, and abundant in goodness and truth.'—Exodus 34:6.

This great event derives additional significance and grandeur from the place in which it stands. It follows the hideous act of idolatry in which the levity and sinfulness of Israel reached their climax. The trumpet of Sinai had hardly ceased to peal, and there in the rocky solitudes, in full view of the mount 'that burned with fire,' while the echoes of the thunder and the Voice still lingered, one might say, among the cliffs, that mob of abject cowards were bold enough to shake off their allegiance to God, and, forgetful of all the past, plunged into idolatry, and wallowed in sensuous delights. What a contrast between Moses on the mount and Aaron and the people in the plain! Then comes the wonderful story of the plague and of Moses' intercession, followed by the high request of Moses, so strange and yet so natural at such a time, for the vision of God's 'glory.' Into all the depths of that I do not need to plunge. Enough that he is told that his desire is beyond the possibilities of creatural life. The mediator and lawgiver cannot rise beyond the bounds of human limitations. But what *can* be *shall* be. God's 'goodness' will pass before him. Then comes this wonderful advance in the progress of divine revelation. If we remember the breach of the Covenant, and then turn to these words, considered as evoked by the people's sin, they become very remarkable. If we consider them as the answer to Moses' desire, they are no less so. Taking these two thoughts with us, let us consider them in—

I. The answer to the request for a sensuous manifestation.

The request is 'show me,' as if some visible manifestation were desired and expected, or, if not a visible, at least a direct perception of Jehovah's glory.' Moses desires that he, as mediator and lawgiver, may have some closer knowledge. The answer to his request is a word, the articulate proclamation of the 'Name' of the Lord. It is higher than all manifestation to sense, which was what Moses had asked. Here there is no symbol as of the Lord in the 'cloud.' The divine manifestation is impossible to sense, and that, too, not by reason of man's limitations, but by reason of God's nature. The manifestation to spirit in full immediate perception is impossible also. It has to be maintained that we know God only 'in part'; but it does not follow that our knowledge is only representative, or is not of Him 'as He is.' Though not whole it is real, so far as it goes. But this is not the highest form. Words and propositions can never reveal so fully, nor with such certitude, as a personal revelation. But we have Christ's life, 'God manifest': not words about God, but the manifestation of the very divine nature itself in action. 'Merciful':—and we see Jesus going about 'doing good.' 'Gracious,' and we see Him welcoming to Himself all the weary, and ever bestowing of the treasures of His love. 'Longsuffering':—'Father! forgive them!' God is 'plenteous in mercy and in truth,' forgiving transgression and sin:—'Thy sins be forgiven thee.'

How different it all is when we have deeds, a human life, on which to base our belief! How much more certain, as well as coming closer to our hearts! Merely verbal statements need proof, they need warming. In Christ's showing us the

Father they are changed as from a painting to a living being; they are brought out of the region of abstractions into the concrete.

'And so the word had breath, and wrought With human hands the creed of creeds.'

'Show us the Father and it sufficeth us.' 'He that hath seen Me, hath seen the Father.'

Is there any other form of manifestation possible? Yes; in heaven there will be a closer vision of Christ—not of God. Our knowledge of Christ will there be expanded, deepened, made more direct. We know not how. There will be bodily changes: 'Like unto the body of His glory.' etc. 'We shall be like Him.' 'Changed from glory to glory.'

II. The answer to the desire to see God's glory.

The 'Glory' was the technical name for the lustrous cloud that hung over the Mercy-seat, but here it probably means more generally some visible manifestation of the divine presence. What Moses craved to see with his eyes was the essential divine light. That vision he did not receive, but what he did receive was partly a visible manifestation, though not of the dazzling radiance which no human eye can see and live, and still more instructive and encouraging, the communication in words of that shining galaxy of attributes, 'the glories that compose Thy name.' In the name specially so-called, the name Jehovah, was revealed absolute eternal Being, and in the accompanying declaration of so-called 'attributes' were thrown into high relief the two qualities of merciful forgiveness and retributive justice. The 'attributes' which separate God from us, and in which vulgar thought finds the marks of divinity, are conspicuous by their absence. Nothing is said of omniscience, omnipresence, and the like, but forgiveness and justice, of both of which men carry analogues in themselves, are proclaimed by the very voice of God as those by which He desires that He should be chiefly conceived of by us. The true 'glory of God' is His pardoning Love. That is the glowing heart of the divine brightness. If so, then the very heart of that heart of brightness, the very glory of the 'Glory of God,' is the Christ, in whom we behold that which was at once 'the glory as of the only begotten of the Father' and the 'Glory of the Father.'

In Jesus these two elements, pardoning love and retributive justice, wondrously meet, and the mystery of the possibility of their harmonious co-operation in the divine government is solved, and becomes the occasion for the rapturous gratitude of man and the wondering adoration of principalities and powers in heavenly places. Jesus has manifested the divine mercifulness; Jesus has borne the burden of sin and the weight of the divine Justice. The lips that said 'Be of good cheer, thy sins be forgiven thee,' also cried, 'Why hast Thou forsaken Me?' The tenderest manifestation of the God 'plenteous in mercy ... forgiving iniquity,' and the most awe-kindling manifestation of the God 'that will by no means clear the guilty,' are fused into one, when we 'behold that Lamb of God that taketh away the sin of the world.'

III. *The answer to a great sin.*

This Revelation is the immediate issue of Israel's great apostasy. Sin evokes His pardoning mercy. This insignificant speck in Creation has been the scene of the wonder of the Incarnation, not because its magnitude was great, but because its need was desperate. Men, because they are sinners, have been subjects of an experience more precious than the 'angels which excel in strength' and hearken 'to the voice of His word' have known or can know. The wilder the storm of human evil roars and rages, the deeper and louder is the voice that peals across the storm. So for us all Christ is the full and final revelation of God's grace. The last, because the perfect embodiment of it; the sole, because the sufficient manifestation of it. 'See that ye refuse not Him that speaketh.'

SIN AND FORGIVENESS

'... Forgiving iniquity and transgression and sin, and that will by no means clear the guilty....'—Exodus 24:7.

The former chapter tells us of the majesty of the divine revelation as it was made to Moses on 'the mount of God.' Let us notice that, whatever was the visible pomp of the external Theophany to the senses, the true revelation lay in the proclamation of the 'Name'; the revelation to the conscience and the heart; and such a revelation had never before fallen on mortal ears. It is remarkable that the very system which was emphatically one of law and retribution should have been thus heralded by a word which is perfectly 'evangelical' in its whole tone. That fact should have prevented many errors as to the relation of Judaism and Christianity. The very centre of the former was 'God is love,' 'merciful and gracious,' and if there follows the difficult addition 'visiting the iniquities,' etc., the New Testament adds its 'Amen' to that. True, the harmony of the two and the great revelation of the *means* of forgiveness lay far beyond the horizon of Moses and his people, but none the less was it the message of Judaism that 'there is forgiveness with Thee that Thou mayest be feared.' The law spoke of retribution, justice, duty, and sin, but side by side with the law was another institution, the sacrificial worship, which proclaimed that God was full of love, and that the sinner was welcomed to His side. And it is the root of many errors to transfer New Testament language about the law to the whole Old Testament system. But, passing away from this, I wish to look at two points in these words.

I. The characteristics of human sins.

II. The divine treatment of them.

I. The characteristics of human sins.

Observe the threefold form of expression—iniquity and transgression and sin.

It seems natural that in the divine proclamation of His own holy character, the sinful nature of men should be characterized with all the fervid energy of such words; for the accumulation even of synonyms would serve a *moral* purpose, expressive at once of the divine displeasure against sin, and of the free full pardon for it in all its possible forms. But the words are very far from all meaning the same thing. They all designate the same actions, but from different points of view, and with reference to different phases and qualities of sin.

Now these three expressions are inadequately represented by the English translation.

'Iniquity' literally means 'twisting,' or 'something twisted,' and is thus the opposite of 'righteousness,' or rather of what is 'straight.' It is thus like our own 'right' and 'wrong,' or like the Latin 'in-iquity' (by which it is happily enough rendered in our version). So looking at this word and the thoughts which connect themselves with it, we come to this:—

(1) All sin of every sort is deviation from a standard to which we ought to be conformed.

Note the graphic force of the word as giving the straight line to which our conduct ought to run parallel, and the contrast between it and the wavering curves into which our lives meander, like the lines in a child's copy-book, or a rude attempt at drawing a circle at one sweep of the pencil. Herbert speaks of

'The crooked wandering ways in which we live.'

There is a path which is 'right' and one which is 'wrong,' whether we believe so or not. There are hedges and limitations for us all. This law extends to the ordering of all things, whether great or small. If a line be absolutely straight, and we are running another parallel to it, the smallest possible wavering is fatal to our copy. And the smallest deflection, if produced, will run out into an ever-widening distance from the straight line. There is nothing which it is more difficult to get into men's belief than the sinfulness of little sins; nothing more difficult to cure ourselves of than the habit of considering quantity rather than quality in moral questions. What a solemn thought it is, that of a great absolute law of right rising serene above us, embracing everything! And this is the first idea that is here in our text—a grave and deep one.

But the second of these expressions for sin literally means 'apostasy,' 'rebellion,' not 'transgression,' and this word brings in a more solemn thought yet, viz.:—

(2) *Every sin is apostasy from or rebellion against God.*

The former word dealt only with abstract thought of a 'law,' this with a 'Lawgiver.'

Our obligations are not merely to a law, but to Him who enacted it. So it becomes plain that the very centre of all sin is the shaking off of obedience to God. Living to 'self' is the inmost essence of every act of evil, and may be as virulently active in the smallest trifle as in the most awful crime.

How infinitely deeper and darker this makes sin to be!

When one thinks of our obligations and of our dependence, of God's love and care, what an 'evil and a bitter thing' every sin becomes!

Urge this terrible contrast of a loving Father and a disobedient child.

This idea brings out the ingratitude of all sin.

But the third word here used literally means 'missing an aim,' and so we come to

(3) Every sin misses the goal at which we should aim. There may be a double idea here—that of failing in the great purpose of our being, which is already partially included in the first of these three expressions, or that of missing the aim which we proposed to ourselves in the act. All sin is a failure.

By it we fall short of the loftiest purpose. Whatever we gain we lose more.

Every life which has sin in it is a 'failure.' You may be prosperous, brilliant, successful, but you are 'a failure.'

For consider what human life might be: full of God and full of joy. Consider what the 'fruits' of sin are. 'Apples of Sodom.' How sin leads to sorrow. This is an inevitable law. Sin fails to secure what it sought for. All 'wrong' is a mistake, a blunder. 'Thou fool!'

So this word suggests the futility of sin considered in its consequences. 'These be thy gods, O Israel!' 'The end of these things is death.'

II. The divine treatment of sins.

'Forgiving,' and yet not suffering them to go unpunished.

(1) God *forgives*, and yet He does not leave sin unpunished, for He will 'by no means *clear* the guilty.'

The one word refers to His love, His heart; the other to the retributions which are inseparable from the very course of nature.

Forgiveness is the flow of God's love to all, and the welcoming back to His favour of all who come. Forgiveness likewise includes the escape from the extreme and uttermost consequences of sin in this life and in the next, the sense of God's displeasure here, and the final separation from Him, which is eternal death. Forgiveness is not inconsistent with retribution. There must needs be retribution, from—

(a) The very constitution of our nature.

Conscience, our spiritual nature, our habits all demand it.

(b) The constitution of the world.

In it all things work under God, but only for 'good' to them who love God. To all others, sooner or later, the Nemesis comes. 'Ye shall eat of the fruit of your doings.'

(2) *God* forgives, and therefore He does not leave sin unpunished. It is divine mercy that strikes. The end of His chastisement is to separate us from our sins.

(3) Divine forgiveness and retributive justice both centre in the revelation of the Cross.

To us this message comes. It was the hidden heart of the Mosaic system. It was the revelation of Sinai. To Israel it was 'proclaimed' in thunder and darkness, and the way of forgiveness and the harmony of righteousness and mercy were veiled. To us it is proclaimed from Calvary. There in full light the Lord passes before us and proclaims, 'I am the Lord, the Lord God merciful and gracious.' 'Ye are come ... unto Jesus.' 'See that ye refuse not Him that speaketh.' 'This is my Beloved Son, hear Him !'

BLESSED AND TRAGIC UNCONSCIOUSNESS

'... Moses wist not that the skin of his face shone while he talked with Him.'—Exodus 34:29.

'... And Samson wist not that the Lord had departed from him.'—Judges 16:20.

The recurrence of the same phrase in two such opposite connections is very striking. Moses, fresh from the mountain of vision, where he had gazed on as much of the glory of God as was accessible to man, caught some gleam of the light which he adoringly beheld; and a strange radiance sat on his face, unseen by himself, but visible to all others. So, supreme beauty of character comes from beholding God and talking with Him; and the bearer of it is unconscious of it.

Samson, fresh from his coarse debauch, and shorn of the locks which he had vowed to keep, strides out into the air, and tries his former feats; but his strength has left him because the Lord has left him; and the Lord has left him because, in his fleshly animalism, he has left the Lord. Like, but most unlike, Moses, he knows not his weakness. So strength, like beauty, is dependent upon contact with God, and may ebb away when that is broken, and the man may be all unaware of his weakness till he tries his power, and ignominiously fails.

These two contrasted pictures, the one so mysteriously grand and the other so tragic, may well help to illustrate for us truths that should be burned into our minds and our memories.

I. Note, then, the first thought which they both teach us, that beauty and strength come from communion with God.

In both the cases with which we are dealing these were of a merely material sort. The light on Moses' face and the strength in Samson's arm were, at the highest, but types of something far higher and nobler than themselves. But still, the presence of the one and the departure of the other alike teach us the conditions on which we may possess both in nobler form, and the certainty of losing them if we lose hold of God.

Moses' experience teaches us that the loftiest beauty of character comes from communion with God. That is the use that the Apostle makes of this remarkable incident in 2 Corinthians 3, where he takes the light that shone from Moses' face as being the symbol of the better luster that gleams from all those who 'behold (or reflect) the glory of the Lord' with unveiled faces, and, by beholding, are 'changed into the likeness' of that on which they gaze with adoration and longing. The great law to which, almost exclusively, Christianity commits the perfecting of individual character is this: Look at Him till you become like Him, and in beholding, be changed. 'Tell me the company a man keeps, and I will tell you his character,' says the old proverb. And what is true on the lower levels of daily life, that most men become assimilated to the complexion of those around them, especially if they admire or love them, is the great principle whereby worship, which is desire and longing and admiration in the superlative degree, stamps the image of the worshipped upon the character of the worshipper. 'They followed after vanity, and have become vain,' says one of the prophets, gathering up into a sentence the whole philosophy of the degradation of humanity by reason of idolatry and the worship of false gods. 'They that make them are like unto them; so is every one that trusteth in them.' The law works upwards as well as downwards, for whom we worship we declare to be infinitely good; whom we worship we long to be like; whom we worship we shall certainly imitate.

Thus, brethren, the practical, plain lesson that comes from this thought is simply this: If you want to be pure and good, noble and gentle, sweet and tender; if you desire to be delivered from your own weaknesses and selfish, sinful idiosyncrasies, the way to secure your desire is, 'Look unto Me and be ye saved, all the ends of the earth.' Contemplation, which is love and longing, is the parent of all effort that succeeds. Contemplation of God in Christ is the master-key that opens this door, and makes it possible for the lowliest and the foulest amongst us to cherish unpresumptuous hopes of being like Him' if we see Him as He is revealed here, and perfectly like Him when yonder we see Him 'as He *is*.'

There have been in the past, and there are today, thousands of simple souls, shut out by lowliness of position and other circumstances from all the refining and ennobling influences of which the world makes so much, who yet in character and bearing, ay, and sometimes in the very look of their meek faces, are living witnesses how mighty to transform a nature is the power of loving gazing upon Jesus Christ. All of us who have had much to do with Christians of the humbler classes know that. There is no influence to refine and beautify men like that of living near Jesus Christ, and walking in the light of that Beauty which is 'the effulgence of the divine glory and the express image of His Person.'

And in like manner as beauty so strength comes from communion with God and laying hold on Him. We can only think of Samson as a 'saint' in a very modified fashion, and present him as an example in a very limited degree. His dependence upon divine power was rude, and divorced from elevation of character and morality, but howsoever imperfect, fragmentary, and I might almost say to our more trained eyes, grotesque, it looks, yet there was a reality in it; and when the man was faithless to his vow, and allowed the crafty harlot's scissors to shear from his head the token of his consecration, it was because the reality of the consecration, rude and external as that consecration was, both in itself and in its consequences, had passed away from him.

And so we may learn the lesson, taught at once by the flashing face of the lawgiver and the enfeebled force of the hero, that the two poles of perfectness in humanity, so often divorced from one another—beauty and strength—have one common source, and depend for their loftiest position upon the same thing. God possesses both in supremest degree, being the Almighty and the All-fair; and we possess them in limited, but yet possibly progressive, measure, through dependence upon Him. The true force of character, and the true power for work, and every real strength which is not disguised weakness, 'a lath painted to look like iron,' come on condition of our keeping close by God. The Fountain is open for you all; see to it that you resort thither.

II. And now the second thought of my text is that the bearer of the radiance is unconscious of it.

'Moses wist not that the skin of his face shone.' In all regions of life, the consummate apex and crowning charm of excellence is unconsciousness of excellence. Whenever a man begins to imagine that he is good, he begins to be bad; and every virtue and beauty of character is robbed of some portion of its attractive fairness when the man who bears it knows, or fancies, that he possesses it. The charm of childhood is its perfect unconsciousness, and the man has to win back the child's heritage, and become 'as a little child,' if he would enter into and dwell in the 'Kingdom of Heaven.' And so in the loftiest region of all, that of the religious life, you may be sure that the more a man is like Christ, the less he knows it; and the better he is, the less he suspects it. The reasons why that is so, point, at the same time, to the ways by which we may attain to this blessed self-oblivion. So let me put just in a word or two some simple, practical thoughts.

Let us, then, try to lose ourselves in Jesus Christ. That way of self-oblivion is emancipation and blessedness and power. It is safe for us to leave all thoughts of our miserable selves behind us, if instead of them we have the thought of that great, sweet, dear Lord, filling mind and heart. A man walking on a tight-rope will be far more likely to fall, if he is looking at his toes, than if he is looking at the point to which he is going. If we fix our eyes on Jesus, then we can safely look, neither to our feet nor to the gulfs; but straight at Him gazing, we shall straight to Him advance. 'Looking off' from ourselves 'unto Jesus' is safe; looking off anywhere else is peril. Seek that self-oblivion which comes from self being swallowed up in the thought of the Lord.

And again, I would say, think constantly and longingly of the unattained. 'Brethren! I count not myself to have apprehended.' Endless aspiration and a stinging consciousness of present imperfection are the loftiest states of man here below. The beholders down in the valley, when they look up, may see our figures against the skyline, and fancy us at the summit, but our loftier elevation reveals untrodden heights beyond; and we have only risen so high in order to discern more clearly how much higher we have to rise. Dissatisfaction with the present is the condition of excellence in all pursuits of life, and in the Christian life even more eminently than in all others, because the goal to be attained is in its very nature infinite; and therefore ensures the blessed certainty of continual progress, accompanied here, indeed, with the sting and bite of a sense of imperfection, but one day to be only sweetness, as we think of how much there is yet to be won in addition to the perfection of the present.

So, dear friends, the best way to keep ourselves unconscious of present attainments is to set our faces forward, and to make 'all experience' as 'an arch wherethro' gleams that untraveiled world to which we move.' 'Moses wist not that the skin of his face shone.'

The third practical suggestion that I would make is, cultivate a clear sense of your own imperfections. We do not need to try to learn our goodness. That will suggest itself to us only too clearly; but what we do need is to have a very clear sense of our shortcomings and failures, our faults of temper, our faults of desire, our faults in our relations to our fellows, and all the other evils that still buzz and sting and poison our blood. Has not the best of us enough of these to knock all the conceit out of us? A true man will never be so much ashamed of himself as when he is praised, for it will always send him to look into the deep places of his heart, and there will be a swarm of ugly, creeping things under the stones there, if he will only turn them up and look beneath. So let us lose ourselves in Christ, let us set our faces to the unattained future, let us clearly understand our own faults and sins.

III. Thirdly, the strong man made weak is unconscious of his weakness.

I do not mean here to touch at all upon the general thought that, by its very nature, all evil tends to make us insensitive to its presence. Conscience becomes dull by practice of sin and by neglect of conscience, until that which at first was as sensitive as the palm of a little child's hand becomes as if it were 'seared with a hot iron.' The foulness of the atmosphere of a crowded hall is not perceived by the people in it. It needs a man to come in from the outer air to detect it. We can accustom ourselves to any mephitic and poisonous atmosphere, and many of us live in one all our days, and do not know that there is any need of ventilation or that the air is not perfectly sweet. The 'deceitfulness' of sin is its great weapon.

But what I desire to point out is an even sadder thing than that—namely, that Christian people may lose their strength because they let go their hold upon God, and know nothing about it. Spiritual declension, all unconscious of its own existence, is the very history of hundreds of nominal Christians amongst us, and, I dare say, of some of us. The very fact that you do not suppose the statement to have the least application to yourself is perhaps the very sign that it does apply. When the lifeblood is pouring out of a man, he faints before he dies. The swoon of unconsciousness is the condition of some professing Christians. Frost-bitten limbs are quite comfortable, and only tingle when circulation is coming back. I remember a great elm-tree, the pride of an avenue in the south, that had spread its branches for more years than the oldest man could count, and stood, leafy and green. Not until a winter storm came one night and laid it low with a crash did anybody suspect what everybody saw in the morning—that the heart was eaten out of it, and nothing left but a shell of bark. Some Christian people are like that; they manage to grow leaves, and even some fruit, but when the storm comes they will go down, because the heart has been out of their religion for years. 'Samson wist not that the Lord was departed from him.'

And so, brother, because there are so many things that mask the ebbing away of a Christian life, and because our own self-love and habits come in to hide declension, let me earnestly exhort you and myself to watch ourselves very narrowly. Unconsciousness does not mean ignorant presumption or presumptuous ignorance. It is difficult to make an estimate of ourselves by poking into our own sentiments and supposed feelings and convictions, and the estimate is likely to be wrong. There is a better way than that. Two things tell what a man is—one, what he wants, and the other, what he does. As the will is, the man is. Where do the currents of your desires set? If you watch their flow, you may be pretty sure whether your religious life is an ebbing or a rising tide. The other way to ascertain what we are is rigidly to examine and judge what we do. 'Let us search and try our ways, and turn again to the Lord.' Actions are the true test of a man. Conduct is the best revelation of character, especially in regard to ourselves. So let us 'watch and be sober'—sober in our estimate of ourselves, and determined to find every lurking evil, and to drag it forth into the light.

Again, let me say, let us ask God to help us. 'Search me, O God! and try me.' We shall never rightly understand what we are, unless we spread ourselves out before Him and crave that Divine Spirit, who is 'the candle of the Lord,' to be carried ever in our hands into the secret recesses of our sinful hearts. 'Anoint thine eyes with eye salve that thou mayest see,' and get the eye salve by communion with God, who will supply thee a standard by which to try thy poor, stained, ragged righteousness. The *collyrium*, the eye salve, may be, will be, painful when it is rubbed into the lids, but it will clear the sight; and the first work of Him, whose dearest name is *Comforter*, is to convince of sin.

And, last of all, let us keep near to Jesus Christ, near enough to Him to feel His touch, to hear His voice, to see His face, and to carry down with us into the valley some radiance on our countenances which may tell even the world, that we have been up where the Light lives and reigns.

'Because thou sayest, I am rich and increased with goods, and have need of nothing, and knowest not that thou art wretched, and miserable, and poor, and blind, and naked, I counsel thee to buy of Me gold tried in the fire, that thou mayest be rich; and white raiment, that thou mayest be clothed, and that the shame of thy nakedness do not appear; and anoint thine eyes with eye salve, that thou mayest see,'

AN OLD SUBSCRIPTION LIST

'And they came, every one whose heart stirred him up, and every one whom his spirit made willing, and they brought the Lord's offering to the work....'
—Exodus 35:21.

This is the beginning of the catalogue of contributions towards the erection of the Tabernacle in the wilderness. It emphasizes the purely spontaneous and voluntary character of the gifts. There was plenty of compulsory work, of statutory contribution, in the Old Testament system of worship. Sacrifices and tithes and other things were imperative, but the Tabernacle was constructed by means of undemanded offerings, and there were parts of the standing ritual which were left to the promptings of the worshipper's own spirit. There was always a door through which the impulses of devout hearts could come in, to animate what else would have become dead, mechanical compliance with prescribed obligations. That spontaneous surrender of precious things, not because a man must give them, but because he delights in letting his love come to the surface and find utterance in giving which is still more blessed than receiving, had but a narrow and subordinate sphere of action assigned to it in the legal system of the Old Covenant, but it fills the whole sphere of Christianity, and becomes the only kind of offering which corresponds to its genius and is acceptable to Christ. We may look, then, not merely at the words of our text, but at the whole section of which they form the introduction, and find large lessons for ourselves, not only in regard to the one form of Christian service which is pecuniary liberality, but in reference to all which we have to do for Jesus Christ, in the picture which it gives us of that eager crowd of willing givers, flocking to the presence of the lawgiver, with hands laden with gifts so various in kind and value, but all precious because freely and delightedly brought, and all needed for the structure of God's house.

I. We have set forth here the true motive of acceptable service.

'They came, every one whose heart stirred him up, and every one whom his spirit made willing.' There is a striking metaphor in that last word. Wherever the spirit is touched with the sweet influences of God's love, and loves and gives back again, that spirit is buoyant, lifted, raised above the low, flat levels where selfishness feeds fat and then rots. The spirit is raised by any great and unselfish emotion. There is buoyancy and glad consciousness of elevation in all the self-sacrifice of love, which dilates and lifts the spirit as the light gas smoothes out the limp folds of silk in a balloon, and sends it heavenwards, a full sphere. Only service or surrender, which is thus cheerful because it is the natural expression of love, is true service in God's sight. Whosoever, then, had his spirit raised and made buoyant by a great glad resolve to give up some precious thing for God's sanctuary, came with his gift in his hand, and he and it were accepted. That trusting of men's giving to spontaneous liberality was exceptional under the law. It is normal under the Gospel, and has filled the whole field, and driven out the other principle of statutory and constrained service and sacrifice altogether. We have its feeble beginnings in this incident. It is sovereign in Christ's Church. There are no pressed men on board Christ's ship. None but volunteers make up His army. 'Thy people shall be willing in the day of Thy might.' He cares nothing for any service but such as it would be pain to keep back; nothing for any service which is not given with a smile of glad thankfulness that we are able to give it.

And for the true acceptableness of Christian service, that motive of thankful love must be actually present in each deed. It is not enough that we should determine on and begin a course of sacrifice or work under the influence of that great motive, unless we renew it at each step. We cannot hallow a row of actions in that wholesale fashion by baptizing the first of them with the cleansing waters of true consecration, while the rest are done from lower motives. Each deed must be sanctified by the presence of the true motive, if it is to be worthy of Christ's acceptance. But there is a constant tendency in all Christian work to slide off its only right foundation, and having been begun 'in the spirit,' to be carried on 'in the flesh.' Constant watchfulness is needed to resist this tendency, which, if yielded to, destroys the worth and power, and changes the inmost nature, of apparently devoted and earnest service.

Not the least subtle and dangerous of these spurious motives which steal in surreptitiously to mar our work for Christ is habit. Service done from custom, and representing no present impulse of thankful devotion, may pass muster with us, but does it do so with God? No doubt a habit of godly service is, in some aspects, a good, and it is well to enlist that tremendous power of custom which sways so much of our lives, on the side of godliness. But it is not good, but, on the contrary, pure loss, when habit becomes mechanical, and, instead of making it easier to call up the true motive, excludes that motive, and makes it easy to do the deed without it. I am afraid that if such thoughts were applied as a sieve to sift the abundant so-called Christian work of the present day, there would be an alarming and, to the workers, astonishing quantity of refuse that would not pass the meshes.

Let us, then, try to bring every act of service nominally done for Christ into conscious relation with the motive which ought to be its parent; for only the work that is done because our spirits lift us up, and our hearts are willing, is work that is accepted by Him, and is blessed to us. And how is that to be secured? How is that glad temper of spontaneous and cheerful consecration to be attained and maintained? I know of but one way. 'Brethren,' said the Apostle, when he was talking about a very little matter—some small collection for a handful of poor people—'ye know the grace of our Lord Jesus Christ, how that, though He was rich, yet for our sakes He became poor, that we, through His poverty, might become rich.' Let us keep our eyes fixed upon that great pattern of and motive for surrender; and our hearts will become willing, touched with the fire that flamed in His. There is only one method of securing the gladness and spontaneousness of devotion and of service, and that is, living very near to Jesus Christ, and drinking in for ourselves, as the very wine that turns to blood and life in our veins, the spirit of that dear Master. Every one whose heart is lifted up will have it lifted up because it holds on by Him who hath ascended up, and who, being 'lifted up, draws all men to Him.' The secret of consecration is communion with Jesus Christ.

The appeal to lower motives is often tempting, but always a mistake. Continual contact with Jesus Christ, and realization of what He has done for us, are sure to open the deep fountains of the heart, and to secure abundant streams. If we can tap these perennial reservoirs they will yield like artesian wells, and need no creaking machinery to pump a scanty and intermittent supply. We cannot trust this deepest motive too much, nor appeal to it too exclusively.

Let me remind you, too, that Christ's appeal to this motive leaves no loophole for selfishness or laziness. Responsibility is all the greater because we are left to assess ourselves. The blank form is sent to us, and He leaves it to our honour to fill it up. Do not tamper with the paper, for remember there is a Returning Officer that will examine your schedule, who knows all about your possessions. So, when He says, 'Give as you like; and I do not want anything that you do not like,' remember that 'Give as you like' ought to mean, 'Give as you, who have received everything from Me, are bound to give.'

II. We get here the measure of acceptable work.

We have a long catalogue, very interesting in many respects, of the various gifts that the people brought. Such sentences as these occur over and over again—'And every man with whom was found' so-and-so 'brought it'; 'And all the women did spin with their hands, and brought that which they had spun'; 'And the rulers brought' so-and- so. Such statements embody the very plain truism that what we have settles what we are bound to give. Or, to put it into grander words, capacity is the measure of duty. Our work is cut out for us by the faculties and opportunities that God has given us.

That is a very easy thing to say, but it is an uncommonly hard thing honestly to apply. For there are plenty of people that are smitten with very unusual humility whenever you begin to talk to them about work. 'It is not in my way,' 'I am not capable of that kind of service,' and so on, and so on. One would believe in the genuineness of the excuse more readily if there were anything about which such people said, 'Well, I *can* do that, at all events'; but such an all-round modesty, which is mostly observable when service is called for, is suspicious. It might be well for some of these retiring and idle Christians to remember the homely wisdom of 'You never know what you can do till you try.' On the other hand, there are many Christians who, for want of honest looking into their own power, for want of what I call sanctified originality, are content to run in the ruts that other people's vehicles have made, without asking themselves whether that is the gauge that their wheels are fit for. Both these sets of people flagrantly neglect the plain law that what we have settles what we should give.

The form as well as the measure of our service is determined thereby. 'She hath done what she could,' said Jesus Christ about Mary. We often read that, as if it were a kind of apology for a sentimental and useless gift, because it was the best that she could bestow. I do not hear that tone in the words at all. I hear, rather, this, that duty is settled by faculty, and that nobody else has any business to interfere with that which a Christian soul, all aflame with the love of God, finds to be the spontaneous and natural expression of its devotion to the Master. The words are the vindication of the form of loving service; but let us not forget that they are also a very stringent requirement as to its measure, if it is to please Christ. 'What she could'; the engine must be worked up to the last ounce of pressure that it will stand. All must be got out of it that can be got out of it. Is that the case about us? We talk about hard work for Christ. Have any of us ever, worked up to the edge of our capacity? I am afraid that if the principles that lie in this catalogue were applied to us, whether about our gold and silver, or about our more precious spiritual and mental possessions, *we* could not say, 'Every man with whom was found' this, that, and the other, 'brought it for the work.'

III. Notice, again, how in this list of offerings there comes out the great thought of the infinite variety of forms of service and offering, which are all equally needful and equally acceptable.

The list begins with 'bracelets, and earrings, and rings, and tablets, all jewels of gold.' And then it goes on to 'blue, and purple, and scarlet, and fine linen, and red skins of rams, and badgers' skins, and shittim wood.' And then we read that the 'women did spin with their hands, and brought that which they had spun'—namely, the same things as have been already catalogued, 'the blue, and purple, and scarlet, and fine linen.' That looks as if the richer gave the raw material, and the women gave the labour. Poor women! they could not give, but they could spin. They had no stores, but they had ten fingers and a distaff, and if some neighbor found the stuff, the ten fingers joyfully set the distaff twirling, and spun the yarn for the weavers. Then there were others who willingly undertook the rougher work of spinning, not dainty thread for the rich soft stuffs whose colors were to glow in the sanctuary, but the coarse black goat's hair which was to be made into the heavy covering of the roof of the tabernacle. No doubt it was less pleasant labour than the other, but it got done by willing hands. And then, at the end of the whole enumeration, there comes, 'And the rulers brought precious stones, and spices, and oil,' and all the expensive things that were needed. The large subscriptions are at the bottom of the list, and the smaller ones are in the place of honour. All this just teaches us this—what a host of things of all degrees of preciousness in men's eyes go to make God's great building!

So various were the requirements of the work on hand. Each man's gift was needed, and each in its place was equally necessary. The jewels on the high-priest's breastplate were no more nor less essential than the wood that made some peg for a curtain, or than the cheap goat's-hair yarn that was woven into the coarse cloth flung over the roof of the Tabernacle to keep the wet out. All had equal consecration, because all made one whole. All was equally precious, if all was given with the same spirit. So there is room for all sorts of work in Christ's great house, where there are not only 'vessels of gold and of silver, but also of wood and of earth,' and all 'unto honour ... meet for the Master's use.' The smallest deed that co-operates to a great end is great. 'The more feeble are necessary.' Every one may find a corner where his special possession will work into the general design. If I have no jewels to give, I can perhaps find some shittim wood, or, if I cannot manage even that, I can at least spin some other person's yarn, even though I have only a distaff, and not a loom to weave it in. Many of us can do work only when associated with others, and can render best service by helping some more highly endowed. But all are needed, and welcomed, and honored, and rewarded. The owner of all the slaves sets one to be a water-carrier, and another to be his steward. It is of little consequence whether the servant be Paul or Timothy, the Apostle or the Apostle's helper. 'He worketh the work of the Lord, as I also do,' said the former about the latter. All who are associated in the same service are on one level.

I remember once being in the treasury of a royal palace. There was a long gallery in which the Crown valuables were stored. In one compartment there was a great display of emeralds, and diamonds, and rubies, and I know not what, that had been looted from some Indian rajah or other. And in the next case there lay a common quill pen, and beside it a little bit of discolored coarse serge. The pen had signed some important treaty, and the serge was a fragment of a flag that had been borne triumphant from a field where a nation's destinies had been sealed. The two together were worth a farthing at the outside, but they held their own among the jewels, because they spoke of brain-work and bloodshed in the service of the king. Many strangely conjoined things lie side by side in God's jewel-cases. Things which people vulgarly call large and valuable, and what people still more vulgarly call small and worthless, have a way of getting together there. For in that place the arrangement is not according to what the thing would fetch if it were sold, but what was the thought in the mind and the emotion in the heart which gave it. Jewels and camel's hair yarn and gold and silver are all massed together. Wood is wanted for the Temple quite as much as gold and silver and precious stones.

So, whatever we have, let us bring that; and whatever we are, let us bring that. If we be poor and our work small, and our natures limited, and our faculties confined, it does not matter. A man is accepted 'according to that he hath, and not according to that he hath not.' God does not ask how much we have given or done, if we have given or done what we could. But He does ask how much we have kept back, and takes strict account of the unsurrendered possessions, the unimproved opportunities, the unused powers. He gives much who gives all, though his all be little; he gives little who gives a part, though the part be much. The motive sanctifies the act, and the completeness of the consecration magnifies it. 'Great' and 'small' are not words for God's Kingdom, in which the standard is not quantity but quality, and quality is settled by the purity of the love which prompts the deed, and the consequent thoroughness of self-surrender which it expresses. Whoever serves God with a whole heart will render to Him a whole strength, and will thus bring Him the gifts which He most desires.

THE COPIES OF THINGS IN THE HEAVENS

'And the Lord spake unto Moses, saying, On the first day of the first month shalt thou set up the tabernacle of the tent of the congregation. And thou shalt put therein the ark of the testimony, and cover the ark with the vail. And thou shalt bring in the table, and set in order the things that are to be set in order upon it; and thou shalt bring in the candlestick, and light the lamps thereof. And thou shalt set the altar of gold for the incense before the ark of the testimony, and put the hanging of the door to the tabernacle. And thou shalt set the altar of the burnt offering before the door of the tabernacle of the tent of the congregation. And thou shalt set the laver between the tent of the congregation and the altar, and shalt put water therein. And thou shalt set up the court round about, and hang up the hanging at the court gate. And thou shalt take the anointing oil, and anoint the tabernacle, and all that is therein, and shalt hallow it, and all the vessels thereof: and it shall be holy. And thou shalt anoint the altar of the burnt offering, and all his vessels, and sanctify the altar: and it shall be an altar most holy. And thou shalt anoint the laver and his foot, and sanctify It. And thou shalt bring Aaron and his sons unto the door of the tabernacle of the congregation, and wash them with water. And thou shalt put upon Aaron the holy garments, and anoint him, and sanctify him; that he may minister unto me in the priest's office. And thou shalt bring his sons, and clothe them with coats: And thou shalt anoint them, as thou didst anoint their father, that they may minister unto me in the priest's office; for their anointing shall surely be an everlasting priesthood throughout their generations.16. Thus did Moses: according to all that the Lord commanded him, so did he.'—Exodus 40:1-16.

The Exodus began on the night after the fourteenth day of the first month. The Tabernacle was set up on the first day of the first month; that is, one year, less a fortnight, after the Exodus. Exodus xix.1 shows that the march to Sinai took nearly three months; and if to this we add the eighty days of Moses' seclusion on the mountain, we get about six months as occupied in preparing the materials for the Tabernacle. 'Setting it up' was a short process, done in a day. The time specified was ample to get ready a wooden framework of small dimensions, with some curtains and coverings of woven stuffs. What a glad stir there would be in the camp on that New Year's day, when the visible token of God's dwelling in its midst first stood there! Our present purpose is simply to try to bring out the meaning of the Tabernacle and its furniture. It was both a symbol and a type; that is, it expressed in material form certain great religious needs and truths; and, just because it did so, it pointed onwards to the full expression and satisfaction of these in Christ Jesus and His gifts. In other words, it was a parable of the requisites for, and the blessings of, communion with God.

Note, then, first, the general lesson of the Tabernacle as a whole. Its name declares its meaning, 'the tent of meeting' (Rev. Ver.). It was the meeting-place of God with man, as the name is explained in Exodus 29:42, 'where I will meet with you, to speak there unto thee.' It is also named simply 'the dwelling'; that is, of God. It was pitched in the midst of the camp, like the tent of the king with his subjects clustered round him. Other nations had temples, like the solemn structures of Egypt; but this slight, movable sanctuary was a new thing, and spoke of the continual presence of Israel's God, and of His loving condescension in sharing their wandering lives, and, like them, dwelling 'within curtains.' It was a visible representation of a spiritual fact for the then present; it was a parable of the inmost reality of communion between man and God; and it was, therefore, a prophecy both of the full realization of His presence among men, in the temple of Christ's body, and of the yet future communion of Heaven, which is set before us by the 'great voice ... saying, Behold, the tabernacle of God is with men.'

The threefold division into court of the worshippers, holy place for the priests, and holiest of all, was not peculiar to the Tabernacle. It signifies the separation which, after all nearness, must still exist. God is unrevealed after all revelation; afar off, however near; shrouded in the utter darkness of the inmost shrine, and only approached by the priestly intercessor with the blood of the sacrifice. Like all the other arrangements of the Sanctuary, the division of its parts declares a permanent truth, which has impressed itself on the worship of all nations; and it reveals God's way of meeting the need by outward rites for the then present, and by the mediation of the great High-Priest in the time to come, whose death rent the veil, and whose life will, one day, make the holiest place in the heavens patent to our feet.

The enumeration of the furniture of the Tabernacle starts from the innermost shrine, and goes outward. It was fit that it should begin with God's special abode. The 'holy of holies' was a tiny chamber, closed in from light, the form, dimensions, materials, and furniture of which were all significant. It measured ten cubits, or fifteen feet, every way, thereby expressing, in its cubical form and in the predominance of the number ten, stability and completeness. It will be remembered that the same cubical form is given to the heavenly city, in the Apocalypse, for the same reason. There, in the thick darkness, unseen by mortals except for the one approach of the high-priest on the day of atonement, dwelt the 'glory' which made light in the darkness, and flashed on the gold which covered all things in the small shrine.

Our lesson does not speak of cherubim or mercy-seat, but specifies only the ark of the testimony. This was a small chest of acacia wood, overlaid with gold, and containing the two tables of the law, which were called the testimony, as bearing witness to Israel of God's will concerning their duty, and as therein bearing witness, too, of what He is. Nor must the other part of the witness-bearing of the law be left out of view,—that it testifies against the transgressors of itself. The ark was the centre-point of the divine revelation, the very throne of God; and it is profoundly significant that its sole contents should be the tables of stone. Egyptian arks contained symbols of their gods, degrading, bestial, and often impure; but the true revelation was a revelation, to the moral sense, of a Being who loves righteousness. Other faiths had their mysteries, whispered in the inmost shrine, which shunned the light of the outer courts; but here the revelation within the veil was the same as that spoken on the house-tops. Our lesson does not refer to the 'mercy seat,' which covered the ark above, and spoke the need for, and the provision of, a means whereby the witness of the law against the worshipper's sins should be, as it were, hid from the face of the enthroned God.

The veil which is referred to in verse 3 was that which hung between the holy of holies and the holy place. It did not 'cover the ark,' as the Authorized Version unfortunately renders, but 'screened' it, as the Revised Version correctly gives it. It blazed with color and embroidered figures of cherubim. No doubt, the colors were symbolical; but it is fancy, rather than interpretation, which seeks meanings beyond splendor in the blue and purple and crimson and white which were blended in its gorgeous folds. What is it which hangs, in ever-shifting hues, between man and God? The veil of creation, embroidered by His own hand with beauty and life, which are symbolized in the cherubim, the types of the animate creation. The two divisions of the Tabernacle, thus separated by the veil, correspond to earth and heaven; and that application of the symbol is certainly intended, though not exclusively.

We step, then, from the mystery of the inner shrine out to the comparatively inferior sacredness of the 'holy place,' daily trodden by the priests. Three articles stand in it: the table for the so-called shew-bread, the great lamp stand, and the golden altar of incense. Of these, the altar was in the midst, right in the path to the holiest place; and on the right, looking to the veil, the table of shew-bread; while on the left was the lamp stand. These three pieces of furniture were intimately connected with each other, and represented various aspects of the spiritual character of true worshippers. The holy place was eminently the people's, just as the most holy place was eminently God's. True, only the priests entered it; but they did so on behalf of the nation. We may expect, therefore, to find special reference to the human side of worship in its equipments; and we do find it. Of the three articles, the altar of incense was in idea, as in locality, the centre; and we consider it first, though it stands last in our list, suggesting that, in coming from the most holy place, the other two would be first encountered. The full details of its construction and use are found in Exodus 30.

Twice a day sweet incense was burned on it, and no other kind of sacrifice was permitted; but once a year it was sprinkled, by the high priest, with expiatory blood. The meaning is obvious. The symbolism of incense as representing prayer in frequent in Scripture, and most natural. What could more beautifully express the upward aspirations of the soul, or the delight of God in these, than the incense sending up its wreaths of fragrant smoke? Incense gives no fragrance nor smoke till it is kindled; and the censer has to be constantly swung to keep up the glow, without which there will be no 'odor of a sweet smell.' So cold prayers are no prayers, but are scentless, and unapt to rise. The heart must be as a coal of fire, if the prayer is to come up before God with acceptance. Twice a day the incense was kindled; and all day long, no doubt, it smoldered, 'a perpetual incense before the Lord.' So, in the life of true communion, there should be daily seasons of special devotion, and a continual glow. The position of the altar of incense was right in the line between the altar of burnt offering, in the outer court, and the entrance to the holiest place; by which we are taught that acceptable prayer follows on reconciliation by sacrifice, and leads into 'the secret place of the Most High.' The yearly atonement for the altar taught that evil imperfection cleaves to all our devotion, which needs and receives the sprinkling of the blood of the great sacrifice.

The great seven-branched candlestick, or lamp stand, stood on the right of the altar, as the priest looked to the most holy place. Its meaning is plain. It is an emblem of the Church as recipient and communicative of light, in all the applications of that metaphor, to a dark world. As the sacred lamps streamed out their hospitable rays into the desert all the night, so God's servants are lights in the world. The lamps burned with derived light, which had to be fed as well as kindled. So we are lighted by the touch of the great Aaron, and His gentle hand tends the smoking wick, and nourishes it to a flame. We need the oil of the Spirit to sustain the light. The lamp was a clustered light, representing in its metal oneness the formal and external unity of Israel. The New Testament unity is of a better kind. The seven candlesticks are made one because He walks in the midst, not because they are welded on to one stem.

Consistency of symbolism requires that the table of shew-bread should, like the altar and the candlestick, express some phase of true worship. Its interpretation is less obvious than that of the other two. The name means literally 'bread of the face'; that is, bread presented to, and ever lying before, God. There are two explanations of the meaning. One sees in the offering only a devout recognition of God as the author of material blessing, and a rendering to Him of His gifts of outward nourishment. In this case, the shew-bread would be anomalous, a literality thrust into the midst of symbolism. The other explanation keeps up the congruity, by taking the material bread, which is the result of God's blessing on man's toil, as a symbol of the spiritual results of God's blessing on man's spiritual toil, or, in other words, of practical righteousness or good works, and conceives that these are offered to God, by a strong metaphor, as acceptable food. It is a bold representation, but we may quote 'I will sup with him' as proof that it is not inadmissible; and it is not more bold than the declaration that our obedience is 'an odor of a sweet smell.' So the three pieces of furniture in the holy place spoke of the true Israel, when cleansed by sacrifice and in communion with God, as instant in prayer, continually raying out the light derived from Him, and zealous of good works, well-pleasing to God.

We pass outwards, through another veil, and stand in the court, which was always open to the people. There, before the door of the Tabernacle, was the altar of burnt offering. The order of our chapter brings us to it last, but the order of worship brought the worshipper to it first. Its distinctive character was that on it the blood of the slain sacrifices was offered. It was the place where sinful men could begin to meet with God, the foundation of all the communion of the inner sanctuary. We need not discuss mere details of form and the like. The great lesson taught by the altar and its place, is that reconciliation is needed, and is only possible by sacrifice. As a symbol it taught every Israelite what his own conscience, once awakened, endorsed, that sin must be expiated before the sinner and God can walk in concord. As prophecy, it assured those whose hearts were touched with longing, that God would Himself 'provide the lamb for the burnt offering,' in some way as yet unknown.

For us it is an intended prefiguration of the great work of Jesus Christ. 'We have an altar.' We need that altar at the beginning of our fellowship with God, as much as Israel did. A Christianity which does not start from the altar of burnt offering will never get far into the holy place, nor ever reach that innermost shrine where the soul lives and adores, silent before the manifest God between the cherubim. The laver, or basin, was intended for the priests' use, in washing hands and feet before ministering at the altar or entering the tabernacle. It teaches the necessity for purity, in order to priestly service.

Thus these three divisions of the Tabernacle and its court set forth the stages in the approach of the soul to God, beginning with the reconciling sacrifice and cleansing water, advancing to closer communion by prayer, impartation of light received, and offering of good works to God, and so entering within the veil into secret sweetness's of union with God, which attains its completeness only when we pass from the holy place on earth to the most holy in the heavens. The remainder of the text can only be glanced at in a sentence or two. It consists of two parts: the consecration of the Tabernacle and its vessels by the anointing oil which, when applied to inanimate objects, simply devoted them to sacred uses, and the consecration of Aaron and his sons.

A fuller account is given in [Leviticus 8](). from which we learn that it was postponed to a later period, and accompanied with a more elaborate ritual than that prescribed here. That consists of three parts: washing, as emblematic of communicated purity; robing, and anointing,—the last act signifying, when applied to men, their endowment with so much of the divine Spirit as fitted them for their theocratic functions. These three things made the 'sanctifying,' or setting apart for God's service, of Aaron and his sons. He is consecrated alone, in order that his primacy may be clearly indicated. He is consecrated by Moses as the higher; then the sons are consecrated with the same ceremonial, to indicate the hereditary priesthood, and the equality of Aaron's successors with himself. 'They truly were many priests, because they were not suffered to continue by reason of death,' and provision for their brief tenure of office was embodied in the consecration of the sons by the side of the father. Their priesthood was only 'everlasting' by continual succession of short-lived holders of the office. But the prediction which closes the text has had a fulfillment beyond these fleeting, shadowy priests, in Him whose priesthood is 'everlasting' and 'throughout all generations.' because 'He ever liveth to make intercession' (Hebrews 7:25).

The Substance and Form of the Breast-Plate and Arrangement of the Twelve Precious Stones.

Ex. 28: 15-21.

Thou shalt make the breast-plate of judgment with cunning work, after the work of the ephod thou shalt make it; of gold, and of blue, and of purple, and of scarlet, and of fine twined linen shalt thou make it. Four-square it shall be, being doubled ; a span shall be the length thereof, and a span shall be the breadth thereof. And thou shalt set in it settings of stones, even four rows of stones: the first row shall be a sardius, (a ruby,) a topaz, and a carbuncle : this shall be the first row. And the second row shall be an emerald, (a chrysoprasus,) a sapphire, and a diamond. And the third row a ligure, (a cyanus,) an agate, and an amethyst. And the fourth row a beryl, (a Tarshish,) and an onyx, and a jasper : they shall be set in gold in their inclosing. And the stones shall be with the names of the children of Israel, twelve, according to their names; like the engravings of a signet, everyone with his name shall they be according to the twelve TRIBES.

In Ex. 39: 8-14, nearly the same words as the preceding are repeated in this chapter; but with this difference, that the former appear in the shape of a command, the latter as the command executed. As the breast-plate of Aaron formed one of the most magnificent appendages to his sacerdotal dress, and at the same time, from the varied brilliancy and translucency of the precious stones, called Urim and Thummim, which were set upon it, was appointed to be the medium whereby responses from heaven were obtained in the Jewish church, it is interesting to examine its construction, and to inquire in what manner the extraordinary effects ascribed to it were produced.

It has been doubted by some whether the breast-plate formed one square, or two squares in one, making an oblong square, because it is described as being four-square doubled: and it has likewise been supposed that the four rows of precious stones, which were set in it, were to be reckoned from right to left in such a manner, that the three stones of each row should be placed laterally, or even with each other. Accordingly some engravings have represented the plate on Aaron's breast, and the rows of stones set upon it, in the way and position just described. But on a more careful examination of the passage above quoted, it will be found that the whole breast-plate was a perfect square, being a span in length and a span in breadth : yet it was a square of a double or twofold character, because it was divided into right and left, to represent a celestial and a spiritual principle : and these again were subdivided, to denote the internal and the external of each: the whole forming four rows in a vertical or upright position, with three stones in each row, and there by representing and signifying the conjunction of all the truths of heaven with the good from which they are derived, and at the same time their high perfection.

The breast-plate itself was made of gold, of blue, and of purple, and of scarlet, and of fine twined linen : its form being that of a square when doubled; it had two rings at the upper ends, and two at the middle of the sides, whereby it was fastened to the ephod: and each of the precious stones, twelve in number, was set in a socket of gold, and had the name of one of the twelve tribes of Israel engraved upon it. Which particular name was inscribed on one stone, and which on another, does not appear from the description given in the Word : and it would be very difficult if not impossible for us at the present day to determine this point, since the order of the names in other parts of the Word varies on different occasions, each name at one time denoting more or less of the good and the true properly signified by it, according to the nature of the subject treated of, the arrangement in each case adopted, and the relation of the one to the other and to the whole.

REPRESENTATION OF THE BREAST-PLATE

With its Precious Stones, their Colors, and Signification

Celestial Love of Good-Celestial Love of Truth
Spiritual Love of Good--Spiritual Love of Truth

With respect to the names appropriated to each stone, it is probable that some one of the preceding orders of nomination was observed, though not particularly stated in the letter of the Word. The order of their birth is generally supposed to have been the order adopted for the breast-plate, probably because that was the order observed on the two onyx-stones placed on the shoulders of the ephod, as in Ex. xxviii. But this being matter of conjecture only, some incline to that arrangement of the tribes, which represented the celestial order subsisting among the angelic societies in heaven, because in their judgment it is the most perfect. Such appears to have been the order of their encampment, as given in Num. ii. 3-21,* when they were arranged according to the four quarters, the standard of the camp of Judah at the head of three tribes being in the east, that of Reuben at the head of three other tribes in the south, that of Ephraim in like manner in the west, and that of Dan in the north, with the camp of the Levites and the tabernacle of the congregation in the midst. For Judah was the first of the tribes, and bore the highest signification; while Dan was the last, and denoted what was lowest in heaven and the church. Similar was the order when they marched, the ark of the covenant going before them, Num. x. 14-28, 33. And probably they were in the same position in relation to the four quarters, as that above described, when Balaam beheld them at a distance, and exclaimed, "How goodly are thy tents, O Jacob, and thy tabernacles, O Israel ! " Num. xxiv. 5.

But as it is possible that some other order than that of encampment may have been required for the breast-plate, which however is not expressed, we shall venture to offer a conjecture on the reason of its being withheld.*

May it not have been, because the names as seen upon the breast-plate in the spiritual world, were not always determined to any one arrangement, but at times shifted from one stone, or from one order of stones, to another, according to the ever-changing circumstances of the church, or of the people who represented the church, either generally or specifically? And as this variety of state was perpetual, and could not have been so well suggested or designated by any fixed order of naming the tribes, may it not have been on this account that the literal sense or the literal record, is silent on the point in question? And yet we are authorized to believe that the names were actually engraved either over, under, or upon the stones in some determinate order, which must therefore have been permanent in the natural world, though variable in the spiritual world. The inconvenience or difficulty which may be supposed to arise from the disagreement here alluded to between what may be called the real fact and the spiritual use to be drawn from the whole description of Urim and Thummim, is entirely obviated by suppressing in the letter all mention of the order of naming the tribes, or the particular application of the names to their respective stones on the breast-plate: which is a peculiarity not exclusively confined to the present case, but may be observed in various other instances to be met with in the Sacred Scriptures both of the Old and the New Testament.

They who are desirous of further information as to facts which really did take place, but which yet were not deemed proper to be admitted as part of the Divine Word, and therefore frequently referred to the books of the Chronicles of the kings of Judah and Israel, (which do not appear to be those books usually called Chronicles, but some others not now extant,) or to some other history collateral with but distinct from the Sacred Volume: see 1 Kings xi. 41; xiv. 19, 29, etc., . Compare also 2 Sam. xx iv. 9, which is a part of the real Word, with 1 Chron. xxi. 5; xxvii. 24, which is no part of the Word, but merely a collateral or supplementary history ; and the variation of the Divine record from what may probably have been the literal fact will immediately appear. Again, compare 2 Kings xxiii. 29, 30, with 2 Chron. xxxv. 20-27 ; and it will be further seen, that several particulars relative to the good king Josiah, which are recorded as facts in the last-mentioned history, are entirely suppressed in the book of Kings, which is a part of the Divine Word.

Similar variations are observable in other historical transactions related in the divine books, when compared with those given in the book of Chronicles : as for example, speaking of the first of David s heroes, it is said in the first book of Chronicles, that " Jashoboam an Hachrnonite, the chief of the captains, lifted up his spear against three hundred, who were slain by him at one time," chap. xi. : but in the second book of Samuel the exploits of the same mighty man are thus described : " The Tachmonite, that sat in the seat, (or, as it might have been rendered, Joshab-bashebeth the Tachmonite,) chief among the captains, the same was Adino the Eznite, he lifted up his spear against eight hundred, whom he slew at one time," chap, xxiii. Here the Divine record makes the number of the slain to be eight hundred, while the collateral history gives only three hundred.

In the New Testament likewise, we find a striking variation in the account given by Matthew, from that in the Acts of the Apostles, concerning the death of Judas. Matt, xxvii. 3-5, states that, after Judas had betrayed Jesus, he repented, returned the thirty pieces of silver, the price of blood, and went and hanged himself. Whereas in the Acts of the Apostles, it is expressly said, that he " purchased a field with the reward of iniquity; and falling headlong, he burst asunder in the midst, and all his bowels gushed out." And it is added, (ver. 19,) that this "was known unto all the dwellers at Jerusalem ; insomuch as that field is called in their proper tongue Aceldama, that is to say, The field of blood." The reader will here observe, that the Evangelist writes by Divine inspiration, and that the Acts of the Apostles is to be regarded only as a collateral history. That the Word should have been so written, as to comprise in its bosom nothing but the divine truths of heaven, while in its external form it selects just so much (and no more) of the Israelites' history, as was found necessary to embody those truths ; and that at the same time the Church should be able to reap from the whole the spiritual benefit intended, is, to the pious and enlightened mind, matter of astonishment, as well as of eternal gratitude.

Since, therefore, the precise arrangement of the names of the twelve tribes, or the distinct appropriation of them to the particular stones of the breast-plate, cannot now be ascertained, and for the reasons above stated need not, it is sufficient for us to know that the stones themselves, together with the names inscribed upon them, represented all the goods and truths of heaven and the church; that those on the right side (of the high-priest) represented the celestial love of good and the celestial love of truth, or in other words, love to the Lord and mutual love; that those on the left represented the spiritual love of good, and the spiritual love of truth, or in other words, charity towards the neighbor and faith from that charity ; while the three stones in each row denoted the perfection and fulness of each kind of love, from its beginning to its end. This signification arises as well from the colors of the stones, as from their number, which was in each row three. We will therefore now consider the rows in their order ; and from the color, transparency and brilliancy of each, endeavor to point out their true signification.

The first Row, consisting of a Ruby, a Topaz, and a Carbuncle

There are two fundamental colors, from which all the rest by combination with each other and with certain degrees of shade or color less media, are derived. These two fundamental colors are red and white; of each of which there are several varieties. The red, being a peculiar display of the primary or most essential quality of fire, is considered in the Sacred Scriptures as expressive of the good of love with which it corresponds: and the white, being a peculiar display of the secondary property of fire, in the same Writings denotes the truth of wisdom with which it also corresponds. Now as the modifications and variegations of natural light with shade produce colors of every description, so the modifications and variegations of spiritual light or truth with ignorance, produce all the varieties of intelligence and wisdom. And hence the precious stones in the breast-plate of Aaron become representative either of higher or of lower degrees of wisdom, (which is always to be understood as inseparable from its love,) according to their brilliancy and transparency, and at the same time according to the kind of light which predominates in them, whether it be red or white. If the red predominate, it is a mark of celestial or most interior affection: but if the white have the ascendancy, then the affection and consequent perception denoted, are of a spiritual or more exterior character.

Under this view of the subject we see the reason why the first row or order, consisting of a ruby, a topaz, and a carbuncle, denotes the celestial love of good, together with its wisdom, namely, because red or flame-colored light predominates and sparkles in each of those stones. The prophet Ezekiel, alluding more particularly to the stones of this order and to their signification as here given, calls them stones of fire, when he addressed the fallen king of Tyrus in these remark able words: " Thus saith the Lord God, Thou sealest up the sum full of wisdom, and perfect in beauty. Thou hast been in Eden the garden of God ; every precious stone was thy covering; thou wast upon the holy mountain of God ; thou hast walked up and down in the midst of the stones of fire. Thou wast perfect in thy ways from the day that thou wast created, till iniquity was found in thee. Thou hast sinned; therefore I will cast thee as profane out of the mountain of God ; and I will destroy thee, O covering cherub, from the midst of the stones of fire," Ezek. xxviii. 12 to 16.

The ruby is a much-admired gem, of a deep red color, with an admixture of purple. In its most perfect and best colored state, it is of exquisite beauty and extreme value. It is often found perfectly pure and free from blemishes and foulness, but much more frequently debased in its value by them, especially in the larger specimens. It is of very great hardness, equal to that of the sapphire and second only to the diamond. It is various in size, but less subject to variations in its shape than most of the other gems, being always of a pebble-like figure, often roundish, sometimes oblong, larger at one end than the other, in some sort resembling a pear, and usually flatted on one side. In general it is naturally so bright and pure on the surface, as to need no polishing ; and when its figure will admit of its being set without cutting, it is often worn in its rough state, and with no other than its native polish. Our jewelers are very nice, though not perfectly determinate, in their distinctions of this gem, knowing it in its different degrees of color under three different names. The first is simply the ruby, the name given it in its deepest colored and most perfect state. The second is the spinal ruby; under this name they comprehend those rubies which are of a somewhat less bright color than the ruby simply so called. The third is the balass ruby ; under which name they express a pale yet a very bright ruby, with a less admixture of the purple tinge than in the deeper colored ones, and of less value. The true ruby comes from the East Indies; and the principal mines of it are in the kingdom of Pegu and the island of Ceylon.

In our common English version of the Bible, instead of the ruby, the translators have named the sardius. But the sardius, being a kind of cornelian verging most frequently to a flesh-color, though sometimes to a blood-red, is neither so valuable nor of so deep a hue as the ruby; and therefore does not so properly answer to the Hebrew word odem, as the ruby does. Some authors call the stone here meant a pyropus, from the resemblance which its color bears to fire or to flame. The modern topaz appears to be a different gem from that of the ancients: and indeed the same may be said of several, if not all, of the other precious stones. That which now bears the name of a topaz may be described as follows: When perfect and free from blemishes, it is considered a very beautiful and valuable gem: it is, however, rarely to be found in this state. It is of a roundish or oblong figure in its native or rough state, usually flatted on one side, and generally of a bright and naturally polished surface, tolerably transparent. They are always of a fine yellow color; but they have this, like the other gems, in several different degrees.

The finest of all are of a true and perfect gold-color, and hence sometimes called chrysolites; but there are some much deeper, and others extremely pale, so as to appear scarcely tinged with yellow. The original topaz emulates the ruby in hardness and the diamond in luster. The most valuable kinds are said to be found in the East Indies; but they are rarely of any great size. The topazes of Peru come next after these in beauty and in value. Those of Europe are principally found in Silesia and Bohemia, but generally with cracks and flaws.

The Hebrew term, pitdah, rendered topaz here and in the English Bible, is, however, by Jerome, Rabbi David, and others, called the emerald, which is a precious stone of a green color, and very different from either of the modern or the ancient topaz. This latter, from its being classed with the ruby and the carbuncle, in all probability exhibited a beautiful flame-colored appearance which in some specimens might also have been enriched with a fine golden tint. To this may be added the circumstance of its being a production of Ethiopia, and not of the places referred to by our modern jewelers. Job, in his estimate of the value of true wisdom, sets it far above rubies, above the topaz of Ethiopia, and above the purest gold, chap, xxviii. 18, 19 ; which is an association that seems to justify our conclusion, that the ruby and the topaz bore an affinity with each other, and jointly with pure gold yielded a most exalted signification.

The carbuncle is a very elegant gem, of a deep red color, with an admixture of scarlet. Its name in the original implies brightness and splendor as of lightning. This gem was known formerly by the name of anthrax. It is said to glitter in the night, and to sparkle much more than the ruby. It is usually found pure and faultless, and is of the same degree of hardness as the sapphire. It is naturally of an angular figure; its usual size is near a quarter of an inch in length, and two-thirds of that in diameter in its thickest part. When held up against the sun, it loses its deep tinge, and becomes exactly of the color of burning charcoal ; whence the propriety of the name which the ancients gave it. It is found in the East Indies, and there but very rarely.

The second row, consisting of a Chrysoprasus, a Sapphire, and a Diamond

This order or row of precious stones denotes the celestial Of truth, together with its wisdom, and answers to the external of the celestial kingdom, as the first row does to its internal.

The stones of the former row derived their signification from their redness ; but the stones of this row derive it from their blueness which partakes of a reddish tinge: for it is to be noted that there is a blue derived from and tinged with red, and likewise a blue derived from and tinged with white. The blue from red, which prevails in the stones of this row, denotes the celestial love of truth; but the blue from white, which prevails in the stones of the next or third row, denotes the spiritual love of good. The affections of the human mind here represented by colors, though not easily discriminated by one who reflects but little upon them, are yet to be considered as distinct from each other, as the stones of the two rows when compared together. In each case the stones appear brilliant and resplendent; but the one kind shows an affinity with red light, and the other an affinity with white light. So likewise of the affections above mentioned, the one has more immediate reference to the good of love, and the other to the truth of wisdom.

The chrysoprasus is described by some as of a pale green color, with an admixture of yellow ; and the name itself seems to imply as much, being compounded of the Greek word chrusos, gold, and prason, a leek. In Hebrew the term is, nophek, which is rendered differently by different translators. Jerome makes it the carbuncle; the Septuagint calls it anthrax ; Onkelos and the English translators, the emerald; and others suppose it to be the ruby. Then comes Rabbi David, who in his book of Roots pronounces it a black precious stone. See Le Dieu in loc. and Leigh's Critica Sacra, 3d edit., 1650. But it is well known, that the gems or precious stones of the ancients differed in many respects from those which bear the same names among the moderns; and therefore nothing can be positively concluded against the nophek of the Scriptures, now called the chrysoprasus, being of a cerulean or blue color with a distant tinge of red.

The sapphire is a pellucid gem, which in its finest state is extremely beautiful and valuable, being nearly equal to the diamond in luster, hardness, and price. Its proper color is a pure blue; in the finest specimens it is of the deepest azure ; in others it varies into paleness in shades of all degrees between that and a pure crystal brightness and water without the least tinge of color, but with a luster much superior to the crystal. It is distinguished into four sorts, viz., the blue sapphire, the white sapphire, the water sapphire, and the milk sapphire. The gem known to us by this name is very different from the sapphire of the ancients, which is said to have been of a deep blue, veined with white, and spotted with small gold-colored spangles, in the form of stars, etc. Moses describes the appearance of heaven under the feet of the God of Israel, to be like a paved work of a sapphire-stone, Ex. xxiv. 10. And the prophet Ezekiel says, that the throne which was in the firmament over the heads of the cherubim, had the appearance of a sapphire-stone, Ezek. i. 26 The ancients had an extraordinary esteem for this stone; and those who wore it about their persons, considered it as a passport to good fortune and happiness. The finest sapphires are brought from Pegu in the East Indies, where they are found in the pebble form, of all the shades of blue. The occidental are from Silesia, Bohemia, and other parts of Europe : but though these are often very beautiful stones, they are greatly inferior both in luster and hardness to the oriental.

The diamond is a clear, bright stone, perfectly translucent, which, though naturally colorless like the purest water, is eminently distinguished from all others of the colorless kind by the luster of its reflections. It derives its name in the original language from its extreme hardness, as it exceeds all the other precious stones in that quality, and can only be cut and ground by its own substance. It is found sometimes in an angular, and sometimes in a pebble-like form : but each kind, when polished, has the same qualities in proportion to its perfection and purity. In its native state it is sometimes bright as if polished by art; but more frequently its surface is obscured with foulnesses of various kinds ; and sometimes it is, as the diamond-cutters call it, veiny, that is, it has certain points inconceivably hard on its surface. Like all other transparent minerals, the diamond is liable to be tinged by metalline particles, and is sometimes found with a cast of red, sometimes blue, sometimes green, and not infrequently yellow. That with a cerulean tinge, delicately announcing its distant affinity with red, appears to have been the diamond that occupied the third place of the second row of precious stones in the breast-plate of judgment. The places whence we obtain the diamond, are the East Indies, particularly the island of Borneo, Visapour, Golconda, and Bengal ; also the Brazils in the West Indies.

The third Row, consisting of a Cyanus, an Agate, and an Amethyst

This row is the first or in most of the spiritual class, and therefore denotes the spiritual love of good: for the two preceding rows represented the internal and the external of the celestial class. By the spiritual love of good is meant charity ; and by the spiritual love of truth is meant faith derived from charity. The stones of this row were of a cerulean or blue color on a white ground ; consequently they were of a distinct order from the stones of the second row, which were likewise cerulean, but on a most delicate red ground.

The cyanus called by Jerome, Josephus, and the English translators, the ligure; by others the lazule, or lapis lazuli; and by Kimchi mistaken for the topaz is a beautiful gem, of a fine blue color, and is found sometimes variegated with spots or clouds of white, and with veins of a shining gold color. But most probably the stone in its pure state is that which is meant in the Sacred Scripture by the cyanus. The agate, or achates, is a valuable gem, variegated with veins and clouds: some having a white ground, some a reddish, some a yellowish, and some again a greenish ground. Cups and vessels are frequently made of agate, which is found in Sicily, Phrygia, and India. The precise color of the stone known among the ancient Jews by the name shebo, which our English translators have rendered the agate, and the German Jews call the topaz, cannot be now ascertained. But from its classification with the other stones of this row, which are known to be cerulean, there is sufficient reason to conclude that this stone also was of the same color, and like them on a white ground, but varying a little from them either in depth of tint or degree of shade.

The amethyst is so called, because in ancient times, when the various charms of superstition were more in vogue than at the present day, it was supposed to be a preservative against drunkenness, or excess in wine; the term in Greek implying as much. But the name in Hebrew, achlamah, is derived from a word which signifies, 1, to dream; 2, to recover from sickness, to grow fat, etc. Aben Ezra says that the stone was so called, because it had the power of causing the person who carried it about with him, to dream. Not to dwell, however, on these and such like fancies, it is sufficient for our present purpose to know, that the gem usually called the amethyst, is of various tints, as purple, violet, blue, etc., and that it is sometimes found nearly colorless, approaching to the purity of the diamond. That which is of a fine cerulean color, with a whitish tinge, appears to be the amethyst of the Sacred Scripture, and the last stone in the third row. They are found in India, Arabia, Armenia, Ethiopia, Cyprus, Germany, Bohemia, and other places: but those from the East are the hardest; and if without spots, they are of the greatest value. They are of various sizes and shapes, from the bigness of a small pea to an inch and a half in diameter.

The fourth Row, consisting of a Tarshish, an Onyx, and a Jasper

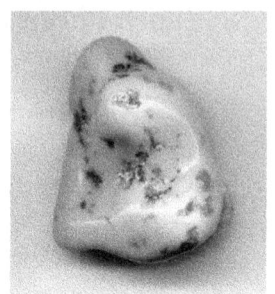

This last row of stones, and second of the spiritual class, Denotes the spiritual love of truth, which is the same thing as the good of faith; the third row as described above, denoting the good of charity. The color of each of the stones of this order approaches to white derived from blue, or to a white with a cerulean tint. The tarshish, called also by the English translators the beryl, and by some the turquoise, the thalassius, and the aqua-marina, is of a sea-blue color, in some fine specimens approaching to white. Some of these stones are a mixture of green and blue resembling sea-water. According to Pliny, there are some which may be called chrysoberyls, on account of their golden or yellow color. These stones are very different from each other with respect to hardness. The oriental are the hardest, and bear the finest polish; and consequently are more beautiful, and of higher value than the occidental. The former kind are found in the East Indies, on the borders of the Euphrates, and at the foot of Mount Taurus. The occidental ones come from Bohemia, Germany, Sicily, the Isle of Elba, etc. And it is affirmed that some of them have been found on the sea-shore.

Tarshish was also the name of a maritime city, mentioned in various parts of the Sacred Scriptures, as in 1 Kings x. 22 ; xxii. 48 ; Ps. xlviii. 7 ; lxxii. 10; Ezek. xxxii. 12, 25; and is supposed to be the same as Tarsus, the birthplace of the apostle Paul. As it appears to have been distinguished for its commerce and wealth, the name of the city was probably given to the precious stone, as well on account of the resemblance of its color to the sea-water off the coast, as because it was usually brought in the ships of Tarshish from one country to another.

The onyx is a much-admired gem, having variously colored zones, but none of them red. In some specimens the zones are beautifully punctuated. In general the onyx resembles the color of a man's nail, being whitish on a cerulean ground.

The jasper is a stone of great variety of colors, often of a beautiful green, and sometimes with spots resembling those of a panther; hence called by some of the rabbies the panther-stone. Jerome identifies it with the beryl. But the true jasper of the ancients, or that which is mentioned in the Sacred Scriptures, (Apoc. xxi. 11 ; Ezek. xxviii. 13,) was neither green nor spotted, but a clear, white, pellucid and brilliant stone, in some degree resembling the crystal for parity and whiteness, yet still discovering its relation to the family of azures, by the distant but easily perceptible tinge of blue, which suffuses all its substance.

The Manner of obtaining Responses from Heaven

In Ancient Times, by Means of the

Twelve Precious Stones called Urim and Thummim.

Having seen what was signified by the twelve precious stones in the breastplate of Aaron, we now come to explain the manner in which responses were given from heaven by their means. We have already stated, and here repeat, that all the diversity of colors in the stones was produced by the modifications and variegations of two fundamental colors proper to light: these are red and white, each in a state of brilliancy and splendor illustrative of their true origin which is fire, and indeed the fire of the sun. From these, through the different degrees of shade, arise all the varieties of color, according to the qualities which different bodies possess of receiving, absorbing, compounding, dividing, reflecting or refracting the incident rays of light. Some bodies also have the property of perverting the rays of light in such a manner, as to extinguish their luster, and to exhibit either a dead white, or a carbonic red, or a variety resulting from the union of these two colors with a gloomy Mack.

These observations equally apply to the rays of spiritual light, which consist of divine truth proceeding from the divine good of the Lord, and illuminating human as well as angelic minds, in the way of mediate as well as immediate influx, according to all the diversities of intelligence and wisdom in each. For every color in the spiritual world is a correspondent expression of some distinct perception of divine truth: and hence it is, that, according to the appearance of colors in that world, their vivid brightness or their fading hue, the various states of wisdom among the inhabitants, which are no other than so many continual revelations from the Lord, are visibly represented. But this was particularly the case when occasions offered during the theocracy established among the Jewish and Israelites' people, for consulting and interrogating the Divine Being by means of Urim and Thummim.

By Urim in the Hebrew language is signified shining fire, or fire which gives forth light: and by Thummim is signified integrity or perfection, which, in reference to the precious stones, must denote their resplendency, brilliancy, and extreme beauty. These were set in the breast-plate which was then called the breast-plate of judgment, the judgment of the children of Israel, and also the judgment of Urim, because thereby responses were given, and divine truths revealed from heaven. The communication thus opened between heaven and the people of Israel through the medium of the high-priest, was at first adopted in conjunction with that direct intercourse with Jehovah which Moses enjoyed during his life; but after the death of Aaron and of Moses, it was established as the usual and regular channel of making known to Jehovah the requests of the people, and of obtaining from Him, in reply, such answers as the Divine Wisdom might dictate.

The manner in which responses were given by means of Urim and Thummim, is not agreed upon by the different writers on the subject. Josephus in his Antiquities says that the twelve precious stones cast forth a more than ordinary luster, when the Israelites were to obtain a victory over their enemies, and that by the appearance or non-appearance of this sign, they judged of the state of their affairs; the luster and brilliancy of the stones foretelling good success, as their appearing dark and cloudy portended nothing but evil. Others are of opinion that the names of the twelve tribes which were engraved on the stones, as also the names of Abraham, Isaac, and Jacob, together with the words shibtey Jeshurun, i. e. the tribes of Jeshurun, or of Israel, added to complete the twenty-two letters of the Hebrew alphabet, were the instruments through which God delivered these oracles. It is therefore supposed that as many of the letters as were requisite to answer the proposed question, raised themselves up above the rest: as for instance, when the Israelites asked the Lord, saying, "Who shall go up for us against the Canaanites first to fight against them?" Judg. i. 1; it was answered by the oracle, "Judah shall go up: behold, I have delivered the land into his hand," ver. 2.

The word Judah, engraved on one of the stones, was raised, and cast forth a great luster; after which the four letters [meaning] *shall go up*, raised themselves on the other stones. But as there is no sufficient authority for this opinion, and as moreover the raised letters in this instance do not give the whole of the answer which was delivered, it is not at all probable that responses were given in this way. The true mode of proceeding and of obtaining answers from heaven on these occasions, appears to have been as follows: The high-priest, (or in his absence, the seer; the prophet, the judge, or the king, whoever it might be that was authorized to put on the ephod, with or without the other appendages of the priesthood,) standing before the ark of the covenant, whether it was in the tabernacle or out of it, and being clothed in all the garments of the sacred office; the MITRE on his head, with the golden plate, the holy crown, in its front; the ephod, the robe, the embroidered coat, and the curious girdle, upon his body;

together with the breast-plate of judgment, having twelve precious stones set in gold, and names engraved thereon of the twelve tribes of the children of Israel, upon his heart ; a solemn appeal was made to Jehovah.

He was literally questioned and interrogated as to the success of undertakings which were meditated; and He was required to make known his will by Urim and Thummim, that is to say, by the sparkling resplendency and vibrations of light from one stone to the other, and at the same time by an audible voice from heaven, or else by a tacit perception corresponding with the splendor of the stones, which might determine the revelation thus communicated to the eye, the ear, and the understanding of the petitioner.

Hence, when the question was put by man, the angels who were present, united in the prayer which with them was entirely of a spiritual character, though with the people of Israel it was merely natural; and as all prayer when genuine, has the power of opening heaven, and thereby of ascending to the Lord himself, a response was immediately given by Divine influx, which became perceptible first to the angels, and afterwards to man through their medium, and the medium of light vibrating in the precious stones. As soon as the angels perceived the Divine will by the resplendent colors presented before their eyes in the spiritual world, (it being one of the prerogatives of their high wisdom to be able to interpret those appearances with the utmost accuracy,) they instantly either infused a suggestion, or gave forth an audible sound expressive of the answer so received by them ; and this voice, which appeared to proceed from off the mercy-seat that was upon the ark of the testimony, from between the two cherubim, (Ex. xxv. 22 ; Num. vii. 89,) was distinctly heard by the priest, the seer, or the prophet, and perhaps by several of the people also who were present, the ears of their spirits being then opened for the express purpose, while the precious stones on the breast-plate were miraculously seen to glitter by the rapid vibrations of light, which were in unison and correspondence with the light or wisdom of heaven.

If the question or interrogation put to Jehovah, spiritually considered, had for its end or object the love and worship of Him alone, in opposition to all other gods and in defiance of all enemies; or if it contemplated the practice and felicity of mutual love, in confirmation or in proof of their love to God; in such cases the vibrations of light most probably commenced either in the first, or in the second row of precious stones, and in imitation of the influx of love into every faculty of the human mind, first successively and then simultaneously pervaded, irradiated, and finally spread a blaze of glory over every part of the breast-plate. And this was an affirmative sign, rendered still more certain and indubitable by the audible voice accompanying it, directing the course they were to take, and thus enjoining them to persevere in that line of duty, which the Divine Wisdom, through the medium of the Word already given, had laid down for their use.

Again, if the question put were in relation to any of the various points of charity and true faith, as weapons of spiritual warfare ; or to speak more literally, if they inquired of Jehovah whether they should proceed against such and such an enemy or not, and whether the event would be successful or unsuccessful; in this case, if they had been previously obedient to the divine commands in other respects, the vibrations of light commenced either in the third, or in the fourth row of stones; and, by pervading and illuminating the whole, gave a positive token of the Divine approbation, which was further confirmed by the audible voice of an angel.

But, on the other hand, if at any time the people of Israel had rebelled, either by relapsing into idolatry, or by other acts of disobedience, and inquiry were made of Jehovah how they were to conduct themselves on any particular emergency, and in the event of their attacking or being attacked by an enemy, whether success would at tend them or not; in this case the luster of the stones was diminished, the vibrations of the light (if any appeared) were irregular, its brilliancy less vivid than usual, and the response given both to the eye and to the ear of the inquirer was of that negative kind, which sufficiently announced the Divine disapprobation, and the consequent failure of the projected enterprise. On some occasions no answer whatever was returned: and therefore it is written, that "when Saul inquired of Jehovah, Jehovah answered him not, neither by dreams, nor by Urim, nor by prophets." 1 Sam. xxviii. 6. General directions for obtaining a response, in regard to Joshua, the successor of Moses, may be seen in Num. xxvii. 18-23.

For affirmative and other responses, and for cases wherein Jehovah refused to give an answer, when inquired of, see Judges xx. 18-28; 1 Sam. x. 22; xiv. 37; xxiii. 2-12; xxviii. 6; xxx. 8; 2 Sam. ii. 1 ; v. 19, 23, 24; 2 Kings iii. 11-19.

Such appears to have been the manner of obtaining responses from heaven among the people of Israel, by means of Urim and Thummim, whenever they were anxious to know the Divine will, or the result of any meditated undertaking. And though to many in the present day it wears the complexion of fable and incredible mystery, yet it ought to be remembered that in the times when it was practiced, almost all the nations of the earth were in the habit of consulting, through the medium of their priests, the demons whom they both feared and worshipped: and it cannot be questioned but they also, on innumerable occasions, received from them such answers, wrap up in artful ambiguity, as still left a conviction in the minds of the inquirers that they were possessed of superhuman wisdom. Of this kind was the famous oracle of Apollo at Delphos, among the heathen Greeks, which, however, with the rest of a similar description, was silenced by the coming of the Lord into the world; at which time the demons or spirits, who acted as familiars to the Pythons and Pythonesses, were removed from their direct association with mankind, and cast into hell.

The Manner of obtaining Responses from Heaven at the Present Day, by Means of the literal Sense of the Word

Extraordinary and wonderful as the preceding account of the manner of obtaining responses from heaven may appear at the present day, it is not more so than the revelation of divine truth in the literal sense of the Word, and particularly the discovery now made of its genuine internal sense by means of the science of correspondences. For as the precious stones in the breast-plate of judgment represented all the truths of heaven, so in like manner they represented all the truths of the Word, but in their literal or external form, and consequently in their effect ; while the different colors arising from the modifications of natural light, denoted the variegations of wisdom and intelligence which may be considered as spiritual light, both in angels and in men.

And as the brilliancy and vibrations of the light in the stones, together with the audible voice from off the mercy-seat, presented both to the eye and to the ear of the person inquiring the desired answer; so the same but a more blessed effect is in our times produced by the extraordinary light of divine truth from the internal sense of the Word, which is spiritually seen to irradiate and as it were to vibrate through every part of its literal sense, while, instead of any external voice being heard, the best affections of the heart are excited, and the Divine will is clearly understood.

In this way we perceive the present use and perpetual application of that part of the Word, which describes the miraculous intercourse between Jehovah and the people of Israel, by means of the breast plate of Urim and Thummim. This intercourse may still be maintained, though not precisely in the same external manner as with the Israelites of old: and yet there is reason to believe that the same internal modifications and variegations of heavenly light which appeared in former times, do now also actually take place in the human mind, on every occasion of consulting the Word purely for the sake of spiritual information and instruction. Thus a person sincerely desirous of knowing the Divine will in relation to any matter either of doctrine or of life, has only to approach the Lord in his Word under a deep sense of his own unworthiness, and an interior acknowledgment that every good gift descends from above. Let him then interrogate the Lord, or inquire of Him, by reading some portion of the Sacred Scriptures for the express purpose of knowing and doing his will; taking care that no improper prejudice or bias of the mind, induced either by education or habits of vice, be suffered to interpose its influence. It is more than probable that the person so reading the Word, or so inquiring of the Lord, will receive an answer most suitable to his state; the pure and radiant light of heaven will appear before his eyes; that is to say, his understanding will be enlightened to discern all necessary truth; the flame of divine love also will be kindled in his bosom; his affections will be still further purified; and he will be supplied with new power to bring his whole life by degrees into complete subjection to the laws of divine order. This conclusion is justified and confirmed by the words of our Lord, " If any man will do his will, he shall know of the doctrine, whether it be of God," John vii. 17.

www.ingramcontent.com/pod-product-compliance
Lightning Source LLC
Chambersburg PA
CBHW081924170426
43200CB00014B/2824